Written by:	James Brown
Editors:	Peter Simunovich, John-Paul Brisigotti
Graphic Design:	Casey Davies
Assistant Writers:	Phil Yates, Andrew Haught, Chris Townley, Nigel Slater, Luke Melia
Assistant Graphic Design:	Sean Goodison, Victor Pesch
Miniatures Design:	Evan Allen, Tim Adcock, Matt Bickley, Will Jaynes
Miniatures Painting:	Aaron Te Hira-Mathie
Cover Art:	Vincent Wai
Internal Art:	Warren Mahy
Proof Readers:	David Adlam, Austin Cheverton, Alexander Costantino, Tom Culpepper, Mark Goddard, Mitch Kemmis, Luke Parsonage, Huw Peregrine-Young, Stephen Smith, Duncan Stradling
Playtest Groups:	Armia Poznań (Bartosz Smarsz), Battleground Club Rostov-on-Don (Alexander Ilyn), Cavalieri dell-Esagono (Eis Annavini), Dad's Army (Gavin Van Rossum), El Tunel (Jose Angel Graña Collazo), La Brigada de Madrid (Jorge Sancho), Maus Haus (Daniel Wilson), Octopus & Friends (Michal Jozwiak), Russians (Ilya Semenov), Wargames Association of Reading (Ian Brook)

**BRITISH FORCES
IN THE DESERT 1942-43**

CONTENTS

THE DESERT RATS

Our mandate from the Prime Minister is to destroy the Axis forces in North Africa. It can be done, and it will be done, beyond any possibility of doubt.

—Field Marshal Bernard Law Montgomery ('Monty')

The North African desert is a harsh and forbidding place. Arid rocky wastes are interspersed with patches of soft sand, where the only vegetation is scattered clumps of desert thorn bushes. Roads are few and poor. In the vast swathes of arid, trackless waste, navigation is often no easier than on a ship at sea, far out of the sight of land. All supplies must be carried to the front by long, straggling supply columns, which are constantly hounded by air attacks. Fuel is always scarce, and even water is a precious resource. It is a brutal environment where only the toughest and most resourceful can survive, let alone fight.

The eyes of the world are on the complex and bloody campaign unfolding in the Western Desert of Egypt and Libya. If the Axis can succeed in pushing the British out of Egypt, there will be nothing keeping them from the rich oil fields of the Middle East, and the strategically vital Suez Canal will open the back door to the Far East. The brave but battered soldiers of the Eighth Army hold the last line of defence against fascist conquest.

The soldiers of the Desert Rats have their own unique flair. The armoured officers gained a reputation for being eccentric in the way that only British gentleman of the Empire-building class can be. Even their manner of dress is flamboyant and stylish, showing little regard for uniform standards. They favour baggy trousers, and brightly coloured silk scarves. They pioneered a style of practical rubber-soled suede desert boots, made for them by cobblers in Cairo, which have still not gone out of fashion to this day.

The tactics of the tank regiments embody the chivalrous traditions of the original cavalry regiments, as they charge headlong into battle like country gentleman riding to a hunt. The fast, lightly-armoured Crusader and Honey tanks can run circles around their slower opposition. The American-built Grant heavy tanks, on the other hand, can sit back and blow the enemy away with their big 75mm guns. Either on their own or in support of the light squadrons, the Grants are a fearsome sight for the German panzers.

The infantry of the motor companies support the armoured forces commendably. Their distinctive khaki drill uniform of short sleeves and baggy shorts symbolises the tough practicality of these hardened desert veterans. On the attack, their job is to beat a path through the enemy minefields and anti-tank defences for the tanks to exploit. In defence, they will steadfastly cling to their patch of desert, digging in and fighting off the enemy with pluck and determination. They call on mortars and Vickers machine-guns to halt the enemy infantry, and their 6-pounder anti-tank guns knock out any Axis tank in the Western Desert.

For artillery cover, the Desert Rats have the excellent Royal Horse Artillery. Their 25-pounder batteries provide outstanding fire support, knocking out the German 88mm anti-tank guns at long range before they can do their deadly work. When things get truly desperate, they are sometimes called on to bolster the anti-tank guns, knocking out German panzers with direct fire. Finally, the dauntless aviators of the RAF's Desert Air Force attack the *Afrika Korps* anywhere, at any time, making sure they can never feel safe.

Are you ready to get stuck in to the enemy with courage, dash and a bit of old-fashioned British stiff upper lip? If you want a highly mobile army, featuring a generous supply of fast tanks backed by excellent infantry and artillery support, then grab your riding crop and a hot cup of tea—the Desert Rats are the army for you.

BRITISH SPECIAL RULES

The following special rules are characteristic of Desert Rats forces, reflecting their own style of equipment, tactics, and approach to battle.

DESERT RATS

The Desert Rats are battered after years of hard fighting, but there is still a lot of fight left in them.

BULLDOG

British infantry are extremely tenacious. They don't like to quit a fight once their blood is up, and once they have fought to capture ground, they won't willingly give it up.

Troops with Bulldog have a better Counterattack rating.

DEADLY

Long-range fire can be very deadly, and is excellent at suppressing infantry forces, but often the decisive action is an old-fashioned bayonet charge. British infantry don't shy away from a hand-to-hand fight. Their training includes ample bayonet drill, and they always have a plentiful supply of Mills Bomb fragmentation hand grenades.

Deadly troops have a better Assault rating.

TANKS

FIGHT ANOTHER DAY

The Eighth Army has been pushed back and forth across the deserts of North Africa more times than they care to count. They still have the stomach for a hard fight, but if the casualties get too high, they will withdraw until they can restart the fight from a more favourable position.

Troops that Fight Another Day have a worse Last Stand rating.

TALLY HO

Armed with guns that struggle to penetrate the enemy armour, and protected by only light armour themselves, the Crusader and Honey tanks of the British light squadrons are a poor match for the German panzers in a toe-to-toe slugging match. Their doctrine revolves around charging straight in close, where short-range fire can threaten the enemy's weaker side armour. This direct style is effective, but does not allow for much tactical subtlety.

Tanks with Tally Ho have a faster Tactical Speed at the cost of a worse Tactics rating.

ARTILLERY

MIKE TARGET

The Royal Artillery have learned the value of concentrating their artillery fire. Different orders indicate the size of the bombardment. A 'Mike target' order calls for the fire of a full regiment of artillery, with 24 guns.

When a Spotting Team successfully Ranges In an Artillery Unit with Mike Target, they may immediately roll to Range In another Artillery Unit. If successful, the second Artillery Unit is treated as Ranging In on the same attempt as the first.

THE WAR SO FAR – 1939 to 1941

SOVIET UNION

Moscow

NORWAY
SWEDEN

ESTONIA
LATVIA
LITHUANIA

Minsk

Kursk

DENMARK
North Sea

Kh

GREAT BRITAIN

POLAND

NETHERLANDS
Berlin
Warsaw

Kiev

London
Dunkirk
BELGIUM
GERMANY

Paris

SLOVAKIA

CRIMEA

FRANCE

HUNGARY

Sevastopol

SWITZERLAND

ROMANIA

Black

VICHY FRANCE

YUGOSLAVIA

BULGARIA

ITALY

ALBANIA

TURKEY

SPAIN

CORSICA
Rome

GREECE

SARDINIA

CRETE

Algiers
Tunis

SICILY

Oran

Mediterranean Sea

TUNISIA
Kasserine Pass

ALGERIA

MOROCCO

Gazala
Tobruk
Mersa Matruh
Alexa

0   500 Km
         500 M

Benghazi
Beda Fomm

El Alamein

Tripoli

LIBYA

EGYPT

El Agheila

Western Front	Eastern Front	North African Theatre	Pacific Theatre

1939

1 September
Germany invades Poland

6 October
Poland Surrenders

3 September
France and Britain declare war on Germany

17 September
Soviet Union invades Poland

1940

9 April - 10 June
Germany invades Denmark and Norway

13 March
Winter War ends. Finland cedes territory

30 November
Winter War begins. Soviet Union invades Finland, but is stopped cold

10 May
Germany invades the Netherlands, Belgium and France

27 May - 5 June
British and French evacuate over 300,000 troops at Dunkirk

28 May
Belgium surrenders

22 June
France surrenders

9 December
Operation Compass. British push Italians back into Libya

13 September
Italy invades Egypt

10 July - 31 October
The Battle of Britain

WAR IN THE DESERT

On 10 June 1940 the Italian dictator Benito Mussolini, known as *Il Duce*, declared war on Great Britain and France. He had dreams of a new Roman Empire, which he would start by kicking the British out of North Africa. In September, Marshal Rodolfo Graziani led a 250,000-strong army out of the Italian colony of Libya into British-held Egypt. The Italian Tenth Army, lacking motorised transport, advanced slowly at the pace of their marching infantry.

The British and Commonwealth defenders, the 30,000-strong Western Desert Force under General Sir Archibald Wavell, were heavily outnumbered and equipped with outdated equipment. They were, however, well trained and determined. Wavell conducted a fighting retreat, his tanks continually harassing and delaying the advancing Italians. Graziani stopped to wait for reinforcements and supplies at Sidi Barrani, less than a quarter of the way to Alexandria, Britain's general headquarters in Africa. There, the Italians dug in, building a series of fortified camps.

When Wavell launched a counteroffensive on 9 December 1940, code-named Operation Compass, its success surprised both the Italians and the British. Wavell's more mobile forces were able to pick off the dispersed Italian positions one by one. What was planned as a five-day raid turned into a general advance, pushing the Italians right back into Libya. The triumphant British captured Bardia and Tobruk before making an ambitious thrust through the desert that cut off the retreating Italians at Beda Fomm, wiping out the Tenth Army. The British suffered fewer than 2000 casualties in Operation Compass, while Italy lost over 130,000 men killed or captured in a campaign lasting two months.

The British advance halted at El Agheila, unable to continue further due to vehicle breakdowns, exhaustion and the long supply line from their base in Egypt. Thinking the Italians beaten, British Prime Minister Winston Churchill redeployed several of the best divisions from Africa to Greece, to help defend against the expected German attack there.

Unfortunately for his plans, a new factor was about to enter the desert war. After the embarrassing defeat of his Italian allies, Hitler was reluctantly forced to either send help or risk facing British domination of the Mediterranean. So, in February 1941, a brilliant commander, *Generalmajor* Erwin Rommel, was sent to Africa at the head of the newly formed *Deutsches Afrika Korps*. With two panzer divisions and motorised support, the *Afrika Korps* was a small, highly-mobile force.

Rommel immediately launched a daring offensive, catching the weakened British off guard. They were driven back from El Agheila in disarray. The German forces swept onward, recapturing Benghazi. In just 12 days, Rommel reversed the tide of the campaign and drove the British back out of Libya apart from the 9th Australian Division and assorted other troops left behind in the port of Tobruk, denying the Axis a vital Mediterranean supply port. The besieged 'Rats of Tobruk' steadfastly resisted everything the Germans and Italians threw at them. They could not break out and escape, but the need to keep them contained made it much harder for Rommel to press his advantage.

The British made two attempts to relieve Tobruk. In May, Operation Brevity recaptured the Halfaya Pass, but the British were thrown back again later the same day. In June, Operation Battleaxe aimed to encircle the Germans, but the *Afrika Korps'* effective use of mobile tank tactics and anti-tank guns—especially the dual-role 88mm gun—repelled the attack with heavy losses. Having failed to lift the siege of Tobruk, Wavell was replaced by General Sir Claude Auchinleck.

Thanks to information received from the Ultra programme, Auchinleck knew Rommel planned to launch a massive attack on Tobruk in November 1941, and made plans to pre-empt him with his own attack. Reinforced and re-supplied, the newly designated Eighth Army now had over 400 tanks, including the speedy new Crusader and the American-built M3 Stuart (which the British nicknamed the 'Honey'). Auchinleck launched Operation Crusader on 18 November, taking the Germans by surprise.

The plan was for the 7th Armoured Division to destroy the Axis panzer force while the infantry pushed through and linked up with the Tobruk defenders. The plan started to unravel when the British tanks were outfought by the *Afrika Korps* at Sidi Rezegh. But the British fought grimly on and eventually, after days of chaotic fighting, Rommel was forced to withdraw. The Tobruk garrison was finally able to break out, joining up with advancing New Zealand troops. Meanwhile, the South Africans re-captured Bardia and Sollum on the Libyan border.

Once again, the Axis front line was pushed back to El Agheila. Operation Crusader proved that the *Afrika Korps* could be beaten, but the Eighth Army had suffered much heavier casualties than their foes.

1941

7 February
Operation Compass ends with the destruction of the Italian Army at Beda Fomm

12 February
Rommel arrives in Libya

22 January
Australians take Tobruk

6 - 30 April
Axis invasion of Yugoslavia and Greece

30 April - 1 May
Rommel assaults Tobruk

4 March
British and Commonwealth forces diverted to Greece

24 March
Rommel attacks in Libya

19 November - 30 December
Operation Crusader: British push Germans and Italians back to El Agheila in Libya.

8 Sept
Siege of Leningrad begins

22 June
Operation Barbarossa: German invasion of Soviet Union begins

2 December
German troops come within sight of the Kremlin in Moscow

5 December
German offensive halted Soviet counter-offensive begins

7 December
Japanese bomb US fleet in Pearl Harbor, Hawaii

THE BATTLE OF GAZALA – 27 MAY 1942

After advancing 800km (500 miles) to El Agheila, it was again the Eighth Army's turn to struggle with the challenges of an overextended supply line. They also overestimated the losses inflicted on the Germans by Operation Crusader. So when Rommel unexpectedly launched Operation Theseus on 21 January 1942, the tired British were caught off guard and driven back. The Axis forces, now designated *Panzer Armee Afrika*, recaptured Benghazi on 28 January.

By 6 February, the Axis advance had been halted and the front line had been stabilised at Gazala, as both sides settled in to rebuild their strength. The British Gazala Line was composed of isolated defensive 'boxes' spread out across the desert, each containing a single brigade defended behind wire, linked by deep minefields. Auchinleck would soon learn, as the Italians had before him, that this tactic did not suit the fluid nature of mobile warfare in the desert. The line stretched 80km (50 miles) from Gazala on the coast, to an old Ottoman fortress at Bir Hakeim, which was held by the 1st Free French Brigade.

On 27 May 1942, Rommel struck again. After a heavy artillery bombardment, the Italian infantry attacked to the north along the narrow coastal road, exactly where the British expected the main attack to come.

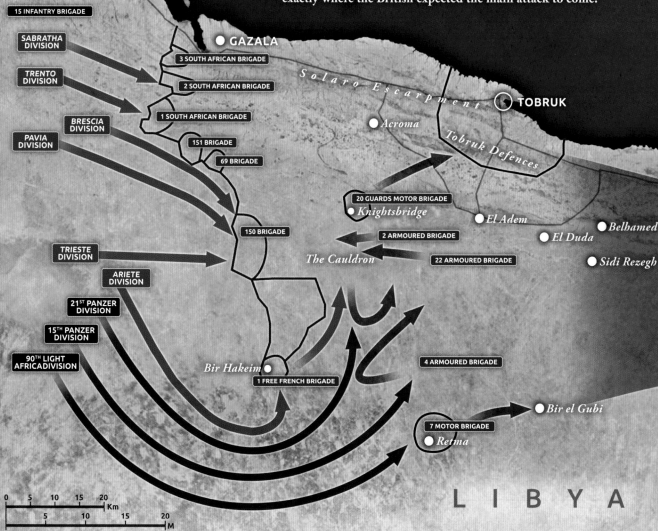

| 15 INFANTRY BRIGADE |
| SABRATHA DIVISION |
| TRENTO DIVISION |
| BRESCIA DIVISION |
| PAVIA DIVISION |
| TRIESTE DIVISION |
| ARIETE DIVISION |
| 21ST PANZER DIVISION |
| 15TH PANZER DIVISION |
| 90TH LIGHT AFRICA DIVISION |

GAZALA

3 SOUTH AFRICAN BRIGADE
2 SOUTH AFRICAN BRIGADE
1 SOUTH AFRICAN BRIGADE
151 BRIGADE
69 BRIGADE
150 BRIGADE

Solaro Escarpment

TOBRUK

Acroma

Tobruk Defences

20 GUARDS MOTOR BRIGADE
Knightsbridge

El Adem

Belhamed
El Duda

2 ARMOURED BRIGADE
The Cauldron
22 ARMOURED BRIGADE

Sidi Rezegh

4 ARMOURED BRIGADE

Bir Hakeim
1 FREE FRENCH BRIGADE

Bir el Gubi

7 MOTOR BRIGADE
Retma

L I B Y A

0 5 10 15 20
Km
5 10 15 20
M

North African Theatre

1 9 4 2

4 February
German advance halted at Gazala

21 January
Operation Theseus: Germans advance from El Agheila

29 January
Axis forces recapture Benghazi

26 May
The Battle of Gazala begins

27 May
Italian Ariete Division besieges 1st Free French Brigade at Bir Hakeim

29 May
Italians clear path through minefields to supply *Afrika Korps*

30 May
Rommel pulls the *Afrika Korps* into a defensive position in 'the Cauldron'

5 June
Operation Aberdeen: British counterattack fails due to miscommunication and mismanagement

10 June
1st Free French Brigade forced to retreat from Bir Hakeim box

11 June
Axis forces begin offensive from the 'Cauldron'

But with characteristic cunning, Rommel sent the bulk of his armoured force south through the supposedly impassable desert, hooking around the southern end of the British line at Bir Hakeim. The speed of the German advance caught the Desert Rats off guard and their scattered Brigades found themselves fighting in isolated pockets. Rommel constantly visited the front lines wherever the fighting was fiercest, personally directing operations and inspiring his troops.

Counting on a quick victory, the attacking panzer units only had enough fuel, food and water for four days. But the Eighth Army was not defeated yet. Determined British counter-attacks from 29 to 31 May put the Axis back on the defensive. Rommel pulled his forces back into a defensive position that would become known as 'the Cauldron', using the Allies' own minefields to protect his rear. The French valiantly hung on in Bir Hakeim, disrupting Rommel's supply line from the south. Although the Italians were able to clear a narrow path to them through the mines, the *Afrika Korps'* supply situation remained desperate. But while the Germans were at their most vulnerable, the British command hesitated.

Rommel wasted no time, throwing his full force against the 150th Brigade box. After determined resistance, the defenders were eventually worn down and forced to surrender, splitting the Gazala Line and finally giving Rommel a clear line of supply.

A major British counterattack on 5 June, Operation Aberdeen, was badly co-ordinated. The initial artillery bombardment fell in the wrong place, leaving the German anti-tank defences unharmed. The advancing British tanks were mauled by expertly placed 88's, leaving their infantry exposed without armoured support. The British suffered heavy casualties—10,000 killed or captured, along with 100 tanks and 120 guns. Rommel was once again free to throw everything he had at the remaining pockets of resistance.

The battered French in Bir Hakeim were finally beaten on 10 June. Many were able to withdraw under cover of darkness and rendezvous with 7th Motor Brigade. With Bir Hakeim finally eliminated, Rommel launched an all-out armoured assault towards El Adem. On 12 June the 201st Guards Brigade was pushed out of the Knightsbridge box. The *Afrika Korps* demonstrated a superiority in tactics, combining tanks with anti-tank guns while on the offensive. The retreating British were pushed back so quickly that they were forced to leave damaged tanks behind. So many tanks were lost on 13 June alone that it became known as 'Black Saturday'. The remaining British armour fell back towards Tobruk, and the Gazala Line was effectively cut off, leaving its remaining defenders no choice but to break out and flee. Auchinleck ordered that Tobruk must be defended at all costs, but by 17 June it was clear that nothing could prevent it from being besieged once again. The British finally withdrew and retreated back across the border into Egypt. With cunning and determination, Rommel had won a crushing victory against superior numbers. Notified that Hitler had promoted him to field marshal, he wrote to his wife, 'I would much rather he had sent me one more division.'

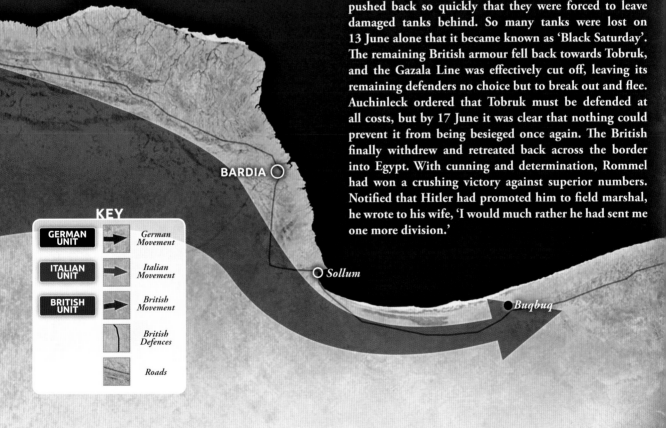

BARDIA ○

KEY

GERMAN UNIT	→	*German Movement*
ITALIAN UNIT	→	*Italian Movement*
BRITISH UNIT	→	*British Movement*
		British Defences
		Roads

○ *Sollum*

● *Buqbuq*

THE FIRST BATTLE OF EL ALAMEIN – 1 JULY 1942

Auchinleck ordered his forces to fall back to defensive positions at Mersa Matruh, where he hoped to stop the Axis advance. The garrison at Tobruk was left to hold on behind the Axis lines, threatening their communication and supply lines as it had in 1941. This time, though, the neglected Tobruk defences had fallen into disrepair, and within a week the defending 2nd South African Division was forced to surrender.

Halfway to Alexandria lay Mersa Matruh, a fortified port town like a smaller Tobruk. A single-track railway terminated there, running through El Alamein to Alexandria. Having learned the limitations of fixed defensive positions, Auchinleck planned to fight a mobile defensive battle, determined to avoid having his forces encircled and captured. But due to poor communication and co-ordination, the British were decisively outmanoeuvred. Rommel captured Mersa Matruh along with 6000 prisoners and a large haul of supplies and equipment, but his main goal of destroying the Eighth Army had narrowly escaped him.

The Eighth Army turned and made a last stand El Alamein, a nondescript railway station on the coast only 60 miles from Alexandria. The British had recognised it as a strong natural defensive position and started to hastily build a fortified line, laying wire and mines. Unlike the Gazala Line, the flanks were secure. The right flank was the sea, and the left flank was the Qattara Depression, a huge, deeply sunken area of salt marshes totally impassible to vehicles. A strong defensive 'box' had been prepared at El Alamein, and weaker ones at Bab el Qattara and Naq Abu Dweis, on the edge of the depression. But most of the 'line' still consisted of open desert. Auchinleck planned for the fortified boxes to split up the attack formations, allowing mobile units to attack their flanks and rear.

The first German units reached the Alamein line on 30 June 1942. Rommel's forces were exhausted by weeks of constant combat without a rest. The supplies captured at Tobruk were helpful, but water and ammunition were still in short supply. Most of their transport vehicles were out of service, and they were only still moving thanks to captured British vehicles. His panzer units were down to only 55 operational tanks, against the British tank strength of 179. Nevertheless, it was now or never for Rommel. He knew that the British position would only get stronger if he didn't attack immediately.

Panzer Armee Afrika's attack began in the pre-dawn darkness of 1 July. Everything in the first day's fighting went in the Eighth Army's favour. The German 90th Light Africa Division found themselves pinned down by the South African artillery firing from the El Alamein box. The 15th and 21st Panzer Divisions were held up all day by determined resistance from 18 Indian Brigade and the 1st Armoured Division at Deir el Shein.

The British were finally learning to match Rommel's mobile tactics. The majority of their strength was divided into mobile brigade groups supported by tanks, as well as the powerful new 6 pdr anti-tank gun, which could penetrate the armour of any of the German panzers. By the end of the first day, the *Afrika Korps* had only 37 tanks left operational. Nevertheless, the British General Staff in Cairo were in a panic, burning confidential documents on 2 July.

Although the British were on the defensive, they spent as much time counterattacking as defending. Wherever possible, Auchinleck tried to strike against the Italians, whose morale was lower than the Germans but whose numbers were critical to holding the Axis line. Much of the bitterest fighting was concentrated on the Ruweisat Ridge, a low stony rise that provided a commanding view for many miles across the surrounding desert. The fierce combat was messy and confusing, and would drag on almost until the end of July. Both armies were at the limit of exhaustion, grimly staying in the fight but too weak to deliver a final knock-out blow.

By 21 July, Rommel was reduced to 26 active tanks and had switched to the defensive. But the Eighth Army was not in much better shape, and was in no position to make a determined counterattack. By 27 July, the First Battle of El Alamein had ended in a stalemate. The Axis push towards Alexandria had been stopped, but it had cost both sides dearly in men and materiel.

Early in August, Prime Minister Churchill personally visited the front lines for five days. Determined to end the Eighth Army's string of defeats, he sacked General Auchinleck and replaced him with the energetic Lieutenant General Bernard Law Montgomery. 'Monty' brought a renewed sense of purpose to his battered but determined forces. Within two weeks, he had eradicated any thought of further retreat and prepared a solid defence against Rommel's next attack.

Monty mounted a carefully planned and executed defensive battle at Alam El Halfa, keeping his armour under tight control. Skilfully placed in hull-down positions, with concentrated support from massed anti-tank guns and artillery, the British tank regiments decimated the attacking panzers and halted Rommel's last-ditch attack in its tracks.

North African Theatre

1942

1 July
German attack begins, and is largely repulsed.
Afrika Korps capture Deir el Shein, losing 18 tanks.

2 July
'Ash Wednesday': in a panic, British General Staff in Cairo burn confidential documents

30 June
Germans arrive at El Alamein Line.
Their first attack is delayed due to supply problems

3 July
Ariete Division attack Ruweisat Ridge from the south

9 July
Litorio Division captures now-abandoned Bab el Qattara box

10 July
9th Australian Division captures Tel el Eisa ridge

10 July
1st South African Division captures Tel el Makh Khad

12 July
21st Panzer Division counterattacks at Tel el Eisa

13 July
21st Panzer Division again fails to capture El Alamein box

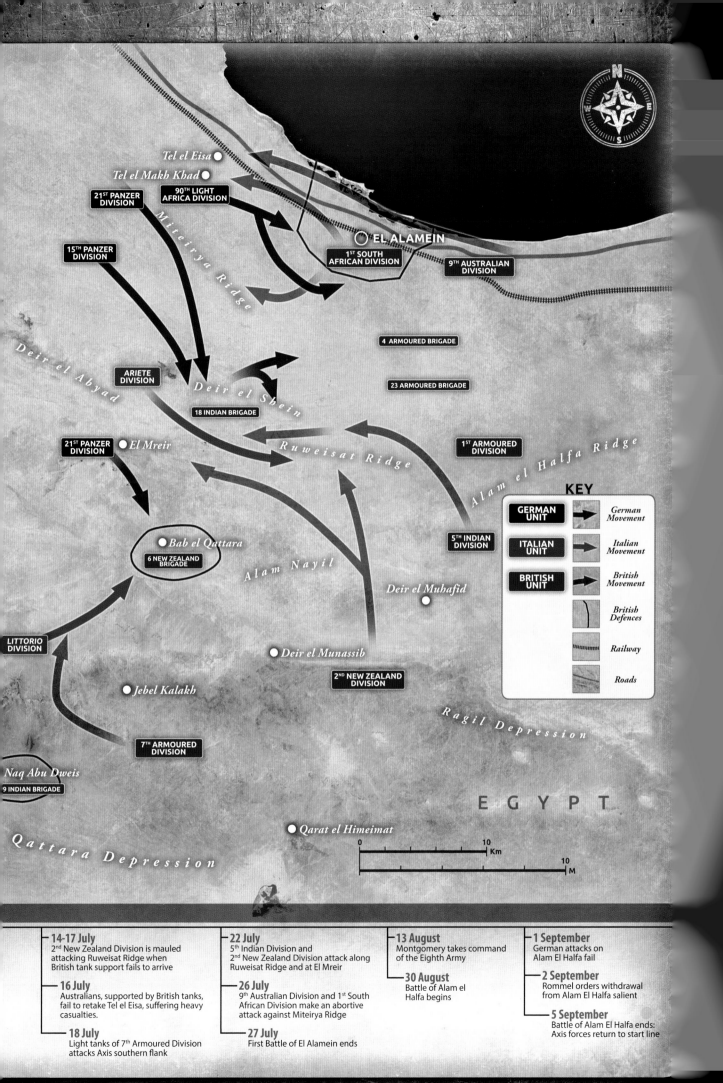

Tel el Eisa

Tel el Makh Khad

21ST PANZER DIVISION

Miteirya Ridge

90TH LIGHT AFRICA DIVISION

15TH PANZER DIVISION

EL ALAMEIN

1ST SOUTH AFRICAN DIVISION

9TH AUSTRALIAN DIVISION

Deir el Abyad

ARIETE DIVISION

Deir el Shein

4 ARMOURED BRIGADE

23 ARMOURED BRIGADE

18 INDIAN BRIGADE

21ST PANZER DIVISION

El Mreir

Ruweisat Ridge

1ST ARMOURED DIVISION

Alam el Halfa Ridge

5TH INDIAN DIVISION

Bab el Qattara

6 NEW ZEALAND BRIGADE

Alam Nayil

Deir el Muhafid

LITTORIO DIVISION

Deir el Munassib

Jebel Kalakh

2ND NEW ZEALAND DIVISION

7TH ARMOURED DIVISION

Ragil Depression

Naq Abu Dweis

9 INDIAN BRIGADE

E G Y P T

Qarat el Himeimat

Qattara Depression

0   10
         Km
         10
         M

KEY

GERMAN UNIT	→	German Movement
ITALIAN UNIT	→	Italian Movement
BRITISH UNIT	→	British Movement
		British Defences
		Railway
		Roads

14-17 July
2nd New Zealand Division is mauled attacking Ruweisat Ridge when British tank support fails to arrive

16 July
Australians, supported by British tanks, fail to retake Tel el Eisa, suffering heavy casualties.

18 July
Light tanks of 7th Armoured Division attacks Axis southern flank

22 July
5th Indian Division and 2nd New Zealand Division attack along Ruweisat Ridge and at El Mreir

26 July
9th Australian Division and 1st South African Division make an abortive attack against Miteirya Ridge

27 July
First Battle of El Alamein ends

13 August
Montgomery takes command of the Eighth Army

30 August
Battle of Alam el Halfa begins

1 September
German attacks on Alam El Halfa fail

2 September
Rommel orders withdrawal from Alam El Halfa salient

5 September
Battle of Alam El Halfa ends: Axis forces return to start line

THE SECOND BATTLE OF EL ALAMEIN – 23 OCT 1942

Again, both sides dug in and rebuilt their strength. Montgomery was under pressure to launch an attack as soon as possible—before the planned Operation Torch landings in November at the latest. The Eighth Army spent six weeks resupplying and rigorously training, each unit carefully rehearsing their part of the upcoming attack. Under the lend-lease programme, President Roosevelt ordered every spare tank to be sent to North Africa. By the start of the battle, Eighth Army had over 1000 tanks, almost double the armoured strength of *Panzer Armee Afrika*.

The Second Battle of El Alamein began on the evening of 23 October. It started with a heavy artillery bombardment all along the line, with almost a thousand guns pounding the German and Italian front lines for half an hour. At zero-hour, 10pm, the attack began. The artillery bombardment did not cease, but instead crept back across the deeper defences, advancing ahead of the attacking infantry—a perfecting of the First World War tactic of the rolling barrage.

The Axis defences stretched back up to 7km (4.5 miles) behind their front lines. The British plan was to attack with infantry, forcing a narrow corridor in the deep Axis minefields, then progressively widen the breach by 'crumbling' the defences on either side. When the German armoured reserve came to the aid of the defenders, the British tanks would be ready to pounce, destroying the outnumbered panzers and breaking out behind enemy lines.

The main thrust would be against the north of the line, with four divisions pushing forward towards Tel el Eisa and Miteirya Ridge. Simultaneous diversionary attacks were launched by the Indians at Ruweisat Ridge and the 7th Armoured Division, supported by the Free French Brigade, at Qaret el Himeimat in the south, aimed at keeping some of the Axis reinforcements away from the main attack.

For several days, the Eighth Army failed to make significant headway. The first, lightly-held, Axis defensive line collapsed quickly, and the infantry were mostly able to push forward to their objectives as planned. However, while the British fought to 'crumble' the successive lines of Axis defences with artillery and localised infantry attacks, their armour repeatedly failed to push through the minefields and anti-tank guns to open ground, where they would be free to manoeuvre.

The British persevered, launching attack after attack in the north, forcing *Panzer Armee Afrika* into a battle of attrition. They began to push a large 'bulge' into the Axis line, centred around a low geographical feature known as 'Kidney Ridge'. Rommel kept up a spirited mobile defence, carefully committing his dwindling panzers wherever they were most needed. A strong Axis counterattack was stopped just south of Kidney Ridge at a position codenamed Outpost Snipe, with two days of desperate defence by the 2nd Battalion of the Rifle Brigade, which destroyed over 50 armoured vehicles at close range with their 6 pdrs.

As the infantry attacks kept up the pressure and continued to crumble the defences, Montgomery began assembling a strong armoured reserve behind the front line, preparing for one last big push, which he hoped would 'hit Rommel for six, right out of Africa'.

This final attack, Operation Supercharge, was launched on 2 November. Again, an overwhelming artillery barrage preceded an attack by the motorised infantry. This time the attackers succeeded in blasting a hole in the exhausted Axis lines, and the next day 1 Armoured Division pushed forward 8km (5 miles) to the Tel El Aqqaqir ridge. There it smashed the last German counterattack. Within days, Rommel ordered a retreat.

El Alamein eradicated the myth of Rommel's invincibility, and it established Montgomery's reputation as a smart, adaptable commander, and a master of the meticulously planned set-piece battle. Churchill finally had the victory he had been waiting for, assuring the British public, 'This is not the end; it is not even the beginning of the end. But it is, perhaps, the end of the beginning.'

Over the next three months the Eighth Army advanced inexorably, recapturing all the territory it had lost, and more. Rommel was pursued back into Libya, and then to Tunisia, where the broken terrain was well-suited to a defiant final defence. Meanwhile a large combined British and US force had landed in Operation Torch and was steadily closing in on Rommel from the west. The Eighth Army soundly defeated Rommel's last offensive in Africa when he tried to delay their advance at Medenine, in southern Tunisia. The Allies would capture the Tunisian capital on 12 May 1943, finally ending the war in North Africa.

North African Theatre

1942

21 September
Exhausted and sick after two years of war, Rommel returns to Germany for medical leave

23 October
Operation Lightfoot: Second Battle of El Alamein begins

24 October
General Stumme, commanding in Rommel's absence, dies of a heart attack while visiting the front lines

25 October
British begin to 'crumble' defences, clearing paths through the minefields

25 October
Major tank battle at Kidney Ridge

25 October
Rommel returns to Africa and resumes command

28-29 October
9th Australian Division attacks on the coast, suffers heavy casualties from an Axis counter-attack

1 November
Axis are almost out of fuel, and have been reduced to 90 operational tanks

2 November
Operation Supercharge: British break through Axis defences

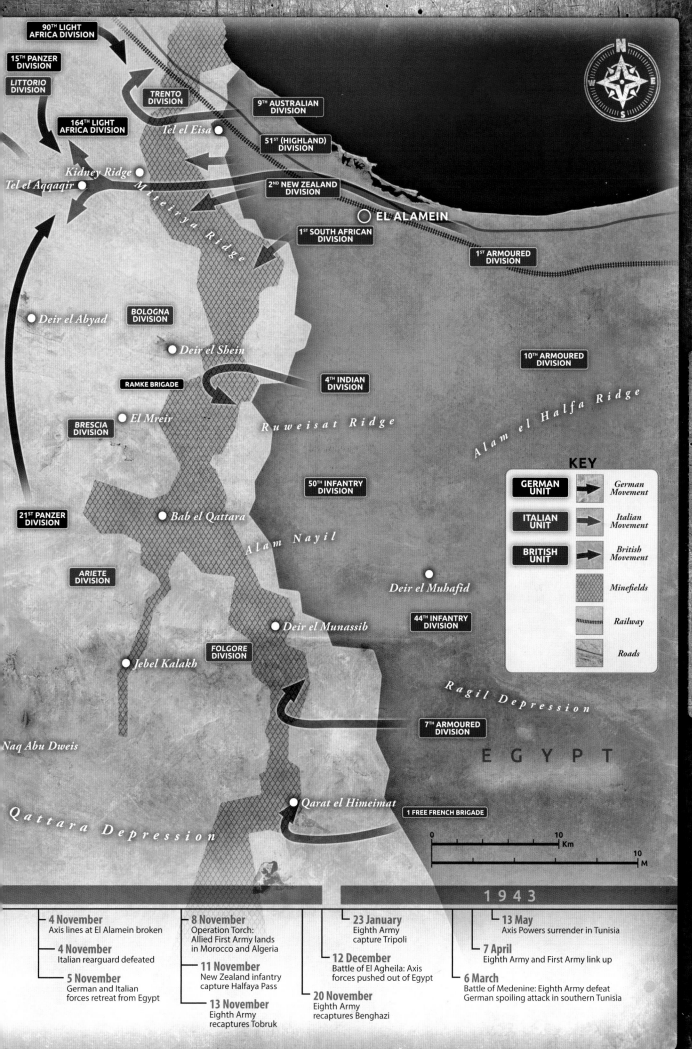

90TH LIGHT AFRICA DIVISION

15TH PANZER DIVISION

LITTORIO DIVISION

TRENTO DIVISION

9TH AUSTRALIAN DIVISION

164TH LIGHT AFRICA DIVISION

Tel el Eisa

51ST (HIGHLAND) DIVISION

Kidney Ridge

Tel el Aqqaqir

2ND NEW ZEALAND DIVISION

Miteirya Ridge

● **EL ALAMEIN**

1ST SOUTH AFRICAN DIVISION

1ST ARMOURED DIVISION

Deir el Abyad

BOLOGNA DIVISION

Deir el Shein

10TH ARMOURED DIVISION

RAMKE BRIGADE

4TH INDIAN DIVISION

Ruweisat Ridge

Alam el Halfa Ridge

BRESCIA DIVISION

El Mreir

50TH INFANTRY DIVISION

KEY

GERMAN UNIT	→	*German Movement*
ITALIAN UNIT	→	*Italian Movement*
BRITISH UNIT	→	*British Movement*
		Minefields
		Railway
		Roads

21ST PANZER DIVISION

Bab el Qattara

Alam Nayil

ARIETE DIVISION

Deir el Muhafid

44TH INFANTRY DIVISION

Deir el Munassib

FOLGORE DIVISION

Jebel Kalakh

Ragil Depression

Naq Abu Dweis

7TH ARMOURED DIVISION

E G Y P T

Qarat el Himeimat

1 FREE FRENCH BRIGADE

0   10 Km

10 M

Qattara Depression

1 9 4 3

4 November
Axis lines at El Alamein broken

4 November
Italian rearguard defeated

5 November
German and Italian forces retreat from Egypt

8 November
Operation Torch: Allied First Army lands in Morocco and Algeria

11 November
New Zealand infantry capture Halfaya Pass

13 November
Eighth Army recaptures Tobruk

23 January
Eighth Army capture Tripoli

12 December
Battle of El Agheila: Axis forces pushed out of Egypt

20 November
Eighth Army recaptures Benghazi

13 May
Axis Powers surrender in Tunisia

7 April
Eighth Army and First Army link up

6 March
Battle of Medenine: Eighth Army defeat German spoiling attack in southern Tunisia

11

KNOW YOUR TANKS

The Desert Rats employed a variety of armoured vehicles, from their own Crusader cruisers to American-built Grant and Honey tanks. Reconnaissance units used light vehicles like the Universal Carrier and Humber armoured car.

BRITISH CRUISER TANKS

The British developed the concept of a cruiser tank to act as fast mechanised cavalry vehicles, in contrast to their infantry tanks, which were slow and heavily armoured, to operate closely with infantry, even under heavy fire. The most numerous British cruiser tank in the Desert War was the Crusader, which entered service in 1941. This first model had an auxiliary machine-gun turret in front of the hull. This was quickly discarded, and slightly thicker armour was added.

CRUSADER II

The Crusader's 2 pdr gun was effective against the lightly-armoured Italian tanks, but when the German panzers arrived it was a different story. The Crusader crews would have to use speed and manoeuvre to survive against the larger guns of the panzers.

Crew (4):	Commander, gunner, loader, driver
Weight:	19.1 tonnes
Length:	5.97m (19' 7")
Width:	2.77m (9' 1")
Height:	2.24m (7' 4")
Weapons:	QF 2 pdr (40mm) gun 7.92mm Besa MG
Armour:	22 - 30mm +18mm
Speed:	42 km/h (26 mph)
Engine:	Nuffield Liberty V12 250 kW (340 hp)

CRUSADER II CS

Making up for the 2 pdr's lack of HE (high explosive) ammunition, the Crusader II CS (Close Support) tank carried a 3-inch (76.2mm) howitzer which could fire high-explosive shells as well as smoke. The Crusader II CS has a shorter, thicker gun barrel than the Crusader II, otherwise they are visually identical.

Crew (4):	Commander, gunner, loader, driver
Weight:	19.1 tonnes
Length:	5.97m (19' 7")
Width:	2.77m (9' 1")
Height:	2.24m (7' 4")
Weapons:	QF 3-inch (76mm) howitzer 7.92mm Besa MG
Armour:	22 - 30mm +18mm
Speed:	42 km/h (26 mph)
Engine:	Nuffield Liberty V12 250 kW (340 hp)

CRUSADER III

The Crusader III entered service in time for the Second Battle of El Alamein. It was up-gunned with the powerful new 6 pdr gun, which packed a decent punch. The larger gun, along with ammunition storage and extra ventilation for the gun fumes, didn't leave enough space in the turret for three men, so the commander also had to act as the loader.

Crew (3):	Commander/loader, gunner, driver
Weight:	20 tonnes
Length:	5.97m (19' 7")
Width:	2.77m (9' 1")
Height:	2.24m (7' 4")
Weapons:	QF 6 pdr (57mm) gun 7.92mm Besa MG
Armour:	27 - 35mm +18mm
Speed:	42 km/h (26 mph)
Engine:	Nuffield Liberty V12 250 kW (340 hp)

LIGHT ARMOURED FIGHTING VEHICLES (AFVs)

UNIVERSAL CARRIER

This versatile little vehicle could be found anywhere the motor battalions went, scouting ahead of the infantry or delivering highly mobile machine-gun support wherever it was needed.

Crew (3):	Commander, gunner, driver
Weight:	3.2 tonnes
Length:	3.65m (12' 0")
Width:	2.06m (6' 9")
Height:	1.57m (5' 2")
Weapons:	.303 Bren light MG
Armour:	4-10mm
Speed:	48 km/h (30 mph)
Engine:	Ford V8 60 kW (80 hp)

HUMBER ARMOURED CAR

The Humber Mk III armoured car was a speedy and reliable wheeled vehicle for the light cavalry regiments, who conducted long-range reconnaissance and raided enemy supply columns.

Crew (3):	Commander, gunner, driver
Weight:	5 tonnes
Length:	4.6m (15' 1")
Width:	2.21m (7' 3")
Height:	2.39m (7' 10")
Weapons:	15mm Besa MG
	7.92mm Besa MG
Armour:	15mm
Speed:	80 km/h (50 mph)
Engine:	Rootes 4L petrol engine 67 kW (90 hp)

AMERICAN-MADE TANKS

HONEY

The speedy M3 Light Tank began the British practice of naming American-supplied tanks after Civil War generals—in this case JEB Stuart. These names were eventually adopted by the US Army as well, but not until after the war.

The Stuart was so reliable and offered such a smooth ride that its crews almost exclusively knew it as the 'Honey' instead.

Crew (4):	Commander, gunner, driver, assistant driver
Weight:	15.2 tonnes
Length:	4.84m (15' 10")
Width:	2.23m (7' 6")
Height:	2.56m (8' 5")
Weapons:	37mm Gun M6
	3x .30-cal Browning MG
Armour:	25-51mm
Speed:	58 km/h (36 mph)
Engine:	Continental R670 164 kW (220 hp)

GRANT

The M3 Medium Tank, which the British named the Grant, was a strange design with its large main gun mounted in the hull, and a smaller secondary gun mounted in a turret. Its crews were very pleased to receive it prior to the Gazala battles of May and June 1942.

Despite its ungainly appearance, it was considered superior to any German tank then in service.

Crew (6):	Commander, turret gunner, driver, turret loader, hull gunner, hull loader
Weight:	27 tonnes
Length:	5.64m (18' 6")
Width:	2.72m (8' 11")
Height:	3.12m (10' 3")
Weapons:	75mm Gun M2
	37mm Gun M5
	3 x Browning .30-cal MG
Armour:	38-51mm
Speed:	42 km/h (26 mph)
Engine:	Continental R975 EC2 300kW (400 hp)

MONTY'S DESERT RATS

To us is given the honour of striking a blow for freedom which will live in history, and in the better days that lie ahead men will speak with pride of our doings.

—Field Marshal Bernard Law Montgomery ('Monty')

The 7th Armoured Division, which would become one of the most famous formations in the Second World War, was formed in 1938 as the Mobile Division in response to mounting Italian aggression in Africa. It began with three Hussar regiments fielding light tanks. The division's first commander, Major-General Percy Hobart, nicknamed them the 'Desert Rats' after the jerboa which is also their insignia.

In February 1940, the Mobile Division became 7th Armoured Division. It was at the forefront of Operation Compass, which drove the Italian Tenth Army out of Egypt. When Rommel's *Afrika Korps* attacked in April 1941, the Desert Rats were busy refitting, but were quickly back in the fight, taking part in Operations Brevity and Battleaxe, attempting to lift the siege of Tobruk.

7th Armoured Division was then reinforced in preparation for Operation Crusader. 22 Armoured Brigade was added, comprising three Yeomanry regiments armed with Crusader tanks, bringing the Division up to a strength of three brigades. Operation Crusader saw some of the most deadly fighting of the Desert campaign. 7th Armoured Division was badly battered by the *Afrika Korps* in the fighting around Sidi Rezegh, but was still able to fight on until the successful but costly conclusion of the offensive.

When Rommel counterattacked once again, 7th Armoured was again refitting, and didn't get back into action until Gazala, where they again fought hard and well. But poor co-ordination between the Army as a whole allowed the Axis forces to knock out its parts piecemeal. The *Afrika Korps* advanced so rapidly that 7th Armoured Division HQ was overrun. General Messervy was captured, but managed to escape the next day.

The division was forced to join the headlong retreat dubbed the 'Gazala Gallop', as British forces struggled to maintain cohesion while falling back to the lines at El Alamein. As the whole Eighth Army began refitting and training for Monty's carefully planned counteroffensive, the division played a major role in defeating Rommel's last-ditch attempt to break the Allied lines at Alam el Halfa.

Once the Second Battle of El Alamein kicked off in October 1942, 7th Armoured Division participated in the armoured breakout codenamed Operation Supercharge. With the Axis forces thrown into full retreat, the division joined the long pursuit back across Egypt and Libya and into Tunisia. In early 1943, the Desert Rats took part in the last push to kick the Axis out of North Africa. On 7 May they entered Tunis, and by 12 May the war in North Africa was over.

7TH ARMOURED DIVISION
XXX CORPS, EIGHTH ARMY, EL ALAMEIN, OCTOBER 1942
Major-General John Harding

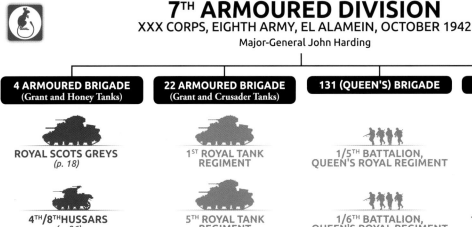

4 ARMOURED BRIGADE (Grant and Honey Tanks)	22 ARMOURED BRIGADE (Grant and Crusader Tanks)	131 (QUEEN'S) BRIGADE	DIVISIONAL SUPPORT

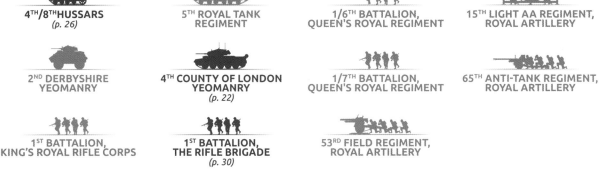

ROYAL SCOTS GREYS (p. 18)

1ST ROYAL TANK REGIMENT

1/5TH BATTALION, QUEEN'S ROYAL REGIMENT

11TH HUSSARS

4TH/8TH HUSSARS (p. 26)

5TH ROYAL TANK REGIMENT

1/6TH BATTALION, QUEEN'S ROYAL REGIMENT

15TH LIGHT AA REGIMENT, ROYAL ARTILLERY

2ND DERBYSHIRE YEOMANRY

4TH COUNTY OF LONDON YEOMANRY (p. 22)

1/7TH BATTALION, QUEEN'S ROYAL REGIMENT

65TH ANTI-TANK REGIMENT, ROYAL ARTILLERY

1ST BATTALION, KING'S ROYAL RIFLE CORPS

1ST BATTALION, THE RIFLE BRIGADE (p. 30)

53RD FIELD REGIMENT, ROYAL ARTILLERY

3RD ROYAL HORSE ARTILLERY

4TH & 97TH FIELD REGIMENTS, ROYAL ARTILLERY

DESERT RATS FORCE

Your Force must contain at least one Formation, and may contain as many Formations as you like.

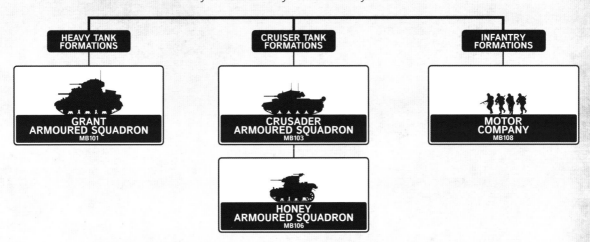

HEAVY TANK FORMATIONS

GRANT ARMOURED SQUADRON
MB101

CRUISER TANK FORMATIONS

CRUSADER ARMOURED SQUADRON
MB103

HONEY ARMOURED SQUADRON
MB106

INFANTRY FORMATIONS

MOTOR COMPANY
MB108

DESERT RATS SUPPORT UNITS

You may field one Support Unit from each box.

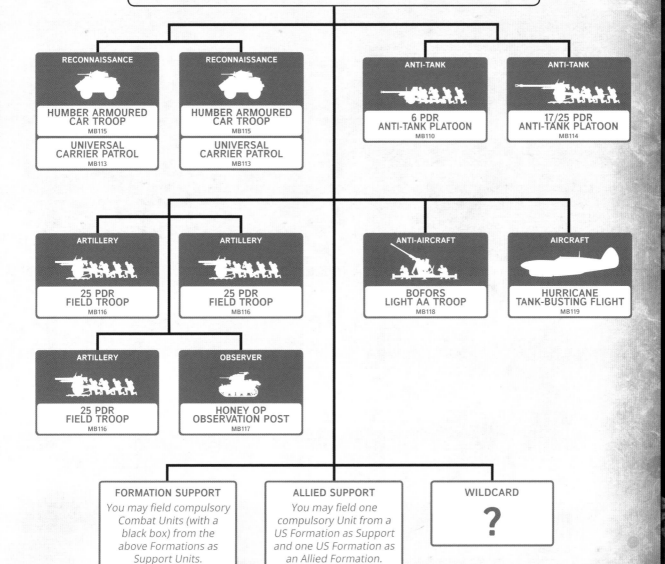

RECONNAISSANCE

HUMBER ARMOURED CAR TROOP
MB115

UNIVERSAL CARRIER PATROL
MB113

RECONNAISSANCE

HUMBER ARMOURED CAR TROOP
MB115

UNIVERSAL CARRIER PATROL
MB113

ANTI-TANK

6 PDR ANTI-TANK PLATOON
MB110

ANTI-TANK

17/25 PDR ANTI-TANK PLATOON
MB114

ARTILLERY

25 PDR FIELD TROOP
MB116

ARTILLERY

25 PDR FIELD TROOP
MB116

ANTI-AIRCRAFT

BOFORS LIGHT AA TROOP
MB118

AIRCRAFT

HURRICANE TANK-BUSTING FLIGHT
MB119

ARTILLERY

25 PDR FIELD TROOP
MB116

OBSERVER

HONEY OP OBSERVATION POST
MB117

FORMATION SUPPORT

You may field compulsory Combat Units (with a black box) from the above Formations as Support Units.

ALLIED SUPPORT

You may field one compulsory Unit from a US Formation as Support and one US Formation as an Allied Formation.

WILDCARD

?

ROYAL SCOTS GREYS

The Royal Scots Greys is one of the oldest cavalry regiments in the British Army, dating back to shortly after the English Civil War. The regiment is most famous for a devastating charge in the Battle of Waterloo, where they crushed the French 45th Regiment, capturing the Eagle which would from then on adorn their regimental badge. Although the regiment unfortunately got caught up in the heat of battle and was counterattacked by French cavalry, suffering heavy losses, what history remembers is the glorious power of what Napoleon later called 'those terrible grey horses'.

The Greys began the Second World War as a horse-mounted cavalry unit stationed in Palestine, helping to police a fragile peace between the Jewish and Arab populations. In February 1940, the regiment conducted its last mounted charge, putting down a civilian riot. It was converted to an armoured regiment in September 1941, receiving intensive tank training in Honeys, before being redeployed to Egypt, where they began learning how to fight in the desert.

In April 1942, the Greys received their first Grant tanks and looked forward to putting them to use. However, after three months of training in the powerful new tanks, the Greys' Grants were instead given to other units urgently needing replacements after the Gazala battles.

By August, the Greys finally had new tanks and were ready for their first taste of armoured warfare as Rommel made a last-ditch attempt to smash the British line at Alam el Halfa. Most of the Eighth Army units that still had functional tanks were concentrated together in one strong brigade, so the Scots Greys found themselves temporarily attached to 22 Brigade. Their Grants were the newest and most mechanically reliable, so were kept back as a mobile reserve.

The defence began according to plan, with the 75mm guns of the Grant tanks inflicting a heavy toll on the attackers. However, the Germans had a new weapon of their own—a new model of Panzer IV up-gunned with a high-velocity long 75mm gun. This proved deadly to the stationary defending Grants, allowing the panzers to punch a hole through the British line.

General 'Pip' Roberts, commanding 22 Brigade, desperately sent the Scots Greys to plug the gap before the panzers could push through, urging them to 'get out their whips.' Just in time, the Greys' Grants crested the ridge and charged down the slope in cavalry fashion, straight into the face of the German attack, which was stopped in its tracks.

In Operation Lightfoot, the opening attack of the Second Battle of El Alamein, the Scots Greys attacked through the minefields in the south, helping to pin 21st Panzer Division and the Italian Ariete Division in place, while the main attack took place in the north. The regiment then joined the break-through in Operation Supercharge, and pursued the retreating Axis across the desert.

ARMOURED DIVISIONS

Three British armoured divisions fought with the Eighth Army in North Africa. The 7th Armoured Division was the first and best known. It was joined by the 1st Armoured Division before the Battle of Gazala in May and June 1942, then by the 10th Armoured Division for the Second Battle of El Alamein in October and November.

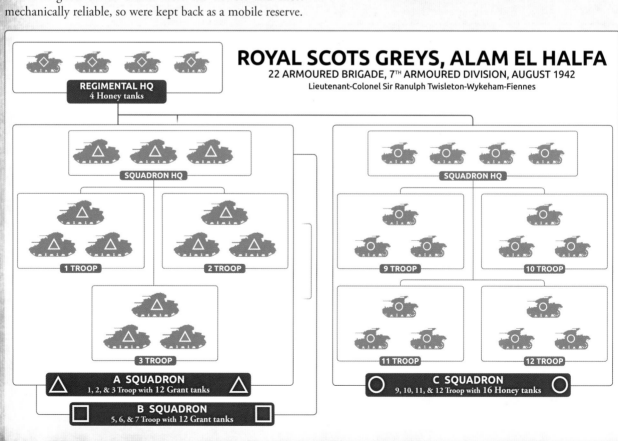

ROYAL SCOTS GREYS, ALAM EL HALFA
22 ARMOURED BRIGADE, 7TH ARMOURED DIVISION, AUGUST 1942
Lieutenant-Colonel Sir Ranulph Twisleton-Wykeham-Fiennes

REGIMENTAL HQ
4 Honey tanks

SQUADRON HQ

1 TROOP **2 TROOP** **3 TROOP**

A SQUADRON
1, 2, & 3 Troop with 12 Grant tanks

B SQUADRON
5, 6, & 7 Troop with 12 Grant tanks

SQUADRON HQ

9 TROOP **10 TROOP** **11 TROOP** **12 TROOP**

C SQUADRON
9, 10, 11, & 12 Troop with 16 Honey tanks

GRANT ARMOURED SQUADRON
HEAVY TANK FORMATION

You must field the Formation HQ and one Combat Unit from each black box.
You may also field one Combat Unit from each grey box.

HEADQUARTERS

GRANT ARMOURED SQUADRON HQ
MB101

ARMOUR

GRANT ARMOURED TROOP
MB102

ARMOUR

GRANT ARMOURED TROOP
MB102

CRUSADER ARMOURED TROOP
MB104 OR MB105

HONEY ARMOURED TROOP
MB107

ARMOUR

GRANT ARMOURED TROOP
MB102

You may field a Combat Unit from a black box as a Support Unit for another Formation.

GRANT ARMOURED SQUADRON HQ

3x Grant (37mm & 75mm) **18 POINTS**
2x Grant (37mm & 75mm) **12 POINTS**

MOTIVATION	
CONFIDENT	**4+**
Fight Another Day **Last Stand**	**5+**
Protected Ammo **Remount**	**3+**

SKILL	
TRAINED	**4+**

• TANK FORMATION •

IS HIT ON	
CAREFUL	**4+**

ARMOUR	
FRONT	**5**
SIDE & REAR	**4**
TOP	**1**

TACTICAL	TERRAIN DASH	CROSS COUNTRY DASH	ROAD DASH	CROSS
10"/25CM	12"/30CM	18"/45CM	20"/50CM	4+

WEAPON	RANGE	ROF HALTED	ROF MOVING	ANTI-TANK	FIRE-POWER	NOTES
Grant Hull (75mm)	24"/60CM	2	1	9	3+	*Forward Firing, Smoke*
Grant Turret (37mm)	24"/60CM	2	1	7	4+	*Secondary Weapon*
Grant (MGs)	16"/40CM	3	3	2	6	

British armoured regiments were delighted to receive the new American-made M3 Grant tank, which gave them a tank with a gun as good as those on the German panzers, with armour to match. Rushed into service to meet the urgent need for a heavy 75mm-armed tank, its clumsy design is a compromise. The main gun is mounted in a hull sponson because no American tank plants could cast a turret big enough for it.

GRANT

FEATURES

BIG GUN: The Grant's 75mm main gun can penetrate 64mm of face-hardened armour, making it deadly to the German panzers. It can also fire high-explosive shells, making up for the main deficiency of the light tanks' smaller guns.

HEAVY ARMOUR: When the British assessed the prototype of the M3, one of the changes they insisted on was the addition of even thicker armour. In comparison to the German panzers, the Grant is as well-protected from the front and even better protected from the sides.

SPECIAL RULES

PROTECTED AMMO: British tank crews have learned from bitter experience how common it is for tanks to explode when hit, due to ammunition fires. One of the modifications they immediately made to their Grants when they received them from the US was to install armoured bins for the ammunition, making them less likely to 'brew up' from an ammunition explosion.

FORWARD FIRING: The sponson for the hull-mounted 75mm gun has limited horizontal traverse, and can only engage targets to the tank's front.

SECONDARY WEAPON: Although each gun has its own gunner and loader, the tank's commander is too busy directing the fire of the main hull-mounted 75mm gun to assist the turret gunner to locate targets for his 37mm gun.

GRANT ARMOURED SQUADRON

GRANT ARMOURED TROOP

3x Grant (37mm & 75mm) | **18 POINTS**

• TANK UNIT •

MOTIVATION	
CONFIDENT	**4+**
Fight Another Day **Last Stand**	**5+**
Protected Ammo **Remount**	**3+**

SKILL	
TRAINED	**4+**

IS HIT ON	
CAREFUL	**4+**

ARMOUR	
FRONT	**5**
SIDE & REAR	**4**
TOP	**1**

The arrival of the Grant in the Battle of Gazala took the Germans by surprise. Its thick armour and powerful 75mm gun are superior to most of the German panzers. Its only real downside is its height, which makes it a conspicuous target in the desert. The placement of the 75mm gun makes it difficult to conceal the tank in a hull-down position behind terrain. At Alam el Halfa, with time to prepare a static defence, the British were able to partly overcome these difficulties by carefully choosing the placement of each Grant.

TACTICAL	TERRAIN DASH	CROSS COUNTRY DASH	ROAD DASH	CROSS
10"/25CM	12"/30CM	18"/45CM	20"/50CM	4+

WEAPON	RANGE	ROF HALTED	ROF MOVING	ANTI-TANK	FIRE-POWER	NOTES
Grant Hull (75mm)	24"/60CM	2	1	9	3+	*Forward Firing, Smoke*
Grant Turret (37mm)	24"/60CM	2	1	7	4+	*Secondary Weapon*
Grant (MGs)	16"/40CM	3	3	2	6	

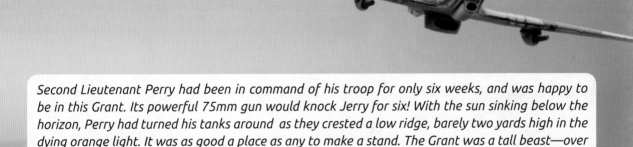

Second Lieutenant Perry had been in command of his troop for only six weeks, and was happy to be in this Grant. Its powerful 75mm gun would knock Jerry for six! With the sun sinking below the horizon, Perry had turned his tanks around as they crested a low ridge, barely two yards high in the dying orange light. It was as good a place as any to make a stand. The Grant was a tall beast—over nine feet—and not easy to hide. Its low gun mount never let the tank go fully 'hull down', exposing only its turret. This spot, though, gave some protection.

It was the longest night of his life, waiting for the dawn. Squinting through his binoculars as the night faded and the sky lightened, he scanned the ridge line three thousand yards away to the southwest, where he expected the enemy to appear. Suddenly, he saw them. Four panzers—the big Mark IVs. They could take a shot any second, but the range was extreme. It was better to wait. Two thousand yards, as the tension weighed heavier on them than the thirty tons of armoured machine in which he and his crew sat.

At fifteen hundred yards the panzers slowed. The German commander in the lead tank, peering through his binoculars, was having trouble seeing with the sun now rising into his eyes. The last thing he saw was the clouds of smoke rising twelve hundred yards in front of him as Second Lieutenant George Perry's troop got their vengeance.

COUNTY OF LONDON YEOMANRY

The 4th County of London Yeomanry (abbreviated 4th CLY) was formed during the build-up of tensions immediately prior to the outbreak of war, around a nucleus of troops split off from its sister regiment, 3rd County of London Yeomanry. The regiment joined 7th Armoured Division as part of 22 Armoured Brigade before the start of Operation Crusader. The operation, the Eighth Army's push to drive the Axis back and liberate Tobruk, was named after the new Crusader tanks which the brigade proudly rode into battle.

The first action of the 4th County of London Yeomanry was against the Italian Ariete Division at Bir El Gubi. One story has it that the regiment's officers went into battle waving riding crops and shouting 'Tally Ho' as they charged the Italian guns. Such valour led to heavy losses, putting the brigade out of battle for several days.

When the Gazala battles started in May 1942, 4th CLY and the rest of 22 Armoured Brigade were back in the desert under the command of the 1st Armoured Division. It helped defend the Knightsbridge Box and was badly battered in the deadly, swirling battles for the 'Cauldron'.

On the first day of the First Battle of El Alamein, the Yeomanry were supporting 18 Indian Brigade against an *Afrika Korps* armoured attack when Lieutenant-Colonel Francis Arkwright was killed by a direct hit from an armour-piercing round. Command of the regiment passed to Major HB Scott.

For the Battle of Alam el Halfa, the depleted regiment temporarily rejoined with 3rd County of London Yeomanry to form 3rd/4th CLY, a composite regiment, as part of 22 Armoured Brigade. The tanks of this composite regiment occupied carefully prepared defensive positions in the rocky foothills. Rather than manoeuvring to meet the advancing enemy, they fought a purely defensive battle. Their Grant tanks were hidden as well as their high profile would allow, holding their fire until the enemy were within close range then inflicting heavy casualties within minutes.

However, the Germans had a new weapon, a new model of Panzer IV mounting a deadly long 75mm gun. This took a heavy toll on the defending Grants. Most of the Grants of A Squadron were 'brewed up', leaving a hole in the British line. The timely arrival of the Scots Greys halted the German attack in the nick of time. The Yeomanry's remaining Crusader tanks were sent to the left of 22 Brigade's position to block a dangerous flanking move by surviving panzers.

After the surrender of the Axis in Tunisia, 4th CLY returned to the United Kingdom with 22 Brigade to prepare for the invasion of Normandy. The regiment's tanks landed on Gold Beach on the night of D-Day, 6 June 1944 and fought in the battles at Villers-Bocage before, after suffering heavy losses of both men and tanks, the regiment was eventually re-amalgamated with its sister regiment in August 1944 as 3rd/4th County of London Yeomanry, serving the rest of the war as part of 4 Armoured Brigade.

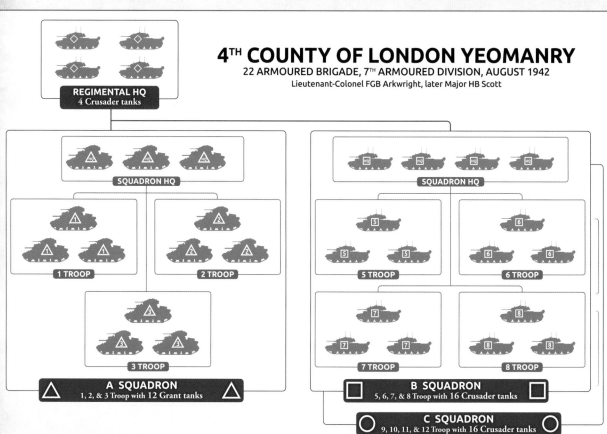

4TH COUNTY OF LONDON YEOMANRY
22 ARMOURED BRIGADE, 7TH ARMOURED DIVISION, AUGUST 1942
Lieutenant-Colonel FGB Arkwright, later Major HB Scott

REGIMENTAL HQ
4 Crusader tanks

SQUADRON HQ

1 TROOP

2 TROOP

3 TROOP

A SQUADRON
1, 2, & 3 Troop with 12 Grant tanks

SQUADRON HQ

5 TROOP

6 TROOP

7 TROOP

8 TROOP

B SQUADRON
5, 6, 7, & 8 Troop with 16 Crusader tanks

C SQUADRON
9, 10, 11, & 12 Troop with 16 Crusader tanks

Geometric symbols painted on the turret sides identify the tank's squadron. The colour of the symbol corresponds to the regiment's position in the brigade (red for the senior regiment, yellow for the second, and blue for the junior regiment) while the shape gives the squadron. Some cavalry regiments also paint troop numbers inside the symbol.

CRUSADER ARMOURED SQUADRON
CRUISER TANK FORMATION

You must field the Formation HQ and one Combat Unit from each black box.
You may also field one Combat Unit from each grey box.

HEADQUARTERS

CRUSADER ARMOURED SQUADRON HQ
MB103

ARMOUR

CRUSADER ARMOURED TROOP
MB104 or MB105

ARMOUR

CRUSADER ARMOURED TROOP
MB104 or MB105

GRANT ARMOURED TROOP
MB102

ARMOUR

CRUSADER ARMOURED TROOP
MB104 or MB105

ARMOUR

CRUSADER ARMOURED TROOP
MB104 or MB105

ARMOUR

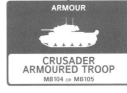

CRUSADER ARMOURED TROOP
MB104 or MB105

You may field a Combat Unit from a black box as a Support Unit for another Formation.

British tank crews raced to load fresh ammunition down through the turret hatches of their Crusaders. When warning cries indicated that the enemy had been sighted, the supply trucks sped off along the powdery track, raising a thick cloud of dust behind them. The blunt shapes of German panzers were advancing in a broad sweep, and the Crusader crews hastily buttoned up, engines roaring as they prepared to engage the veteran Afrika Korps tanks. The recently-arrived Crusader cruisers had proved to be fast at covering ground and quick to get their 2-pounder guns laid on target.

The Crusaders accelerated over the stony plain, their gunners beginning to fire. The Mk III panzers responded in kind and fiery columns of black smoke began to mark losses for both sides. The British tanks attempted to close the range, heading straight at the panzers. Trading fire at long range did no favours for the lighter armour of the British tanks, as they instead sought to engage the Germans in a mobile duel, using their superior speed to keep the enemy off balance, pumping out a steady tempo of rounds as they raced through the German formation.

The British tanks pressed forward to get in a few more flank shots as the Panzers withdrew, brewing up one more enemy tank before being recalled. Hard experience had tutored the cruiser tank crews not to pursue the panzers into the inevitable anti-tank gun ambush.

CRUSADER ARMOURED SQUADRON HQ

2x Crusader II (2 pdr)
2x Crusader CS (3 inch) **7 POINTS**

1x Crusader II (2 pdr)
2x Crusader CS (3 inch) **5 POINTS**

• TANK FORMATION •

IS HIT ON
AGGRESSIVE 3+

ARMOUR
FRONT 3
SIDE & REAR 2
TOP 1

The light squadrons of the armoured regiments embody the dash and daring of the British cavalry. Fast and manoeuvrable but not as heavily armoured as the enemy panzers, they use speed and cover to protect themselves. They are often relegated to scouting or protecting the flanks of the regiment while their heavy cousins, the Grants, take the fight to the enemy.

TACTICAL	TERRAIN DASH	CROSS COUNTRY DASH	ROAD DASH	CROSS
14"/35cm	14"/35cm	20"/50cm	24"/60cm	3+

WEAPON	RANGE	ROF HALTED	MOVING	ANTI-TANK	FIRE-POWER	NOTES
Crusader II (2 pdr)	24"/60cm	2	1	7	4+	*No HE*
Crusader CS (3-inch)	32"/80cm	ARTILLERY		2	4+	*Smoke Bombardment*
or Direct Fire	16"/40cm	2	1	5	3+	*Smoke*
Crusader II & CS (MG)	16"/40cm	3	3	2	6	

CRUSADERS

CRUSADER II FEATURES

HIGH SPEED: Cruiser tanks are the sports cars of the tank world. The Crusader's excellent power-to-weight ratio and smooth Christie suspension give it excellent cross-country performance.

TACTICAL SPEED: The Crusader is designed especially for the fast-moving and aggressive fighting style which the British tankers are trained for. The gunner can aim quickly while the tank is moving. He raises and lowers the gun with his shoulder, while using the turret's fast hydraulic traverse system to track the target. Its large turret gives the crew room to operate effectively.

CRUSADER II CS FEATURES

ARTILLERY: Each squadron has a few Crusader CS (Close Support) tanks, which have their main gun replaced with a 3-inch howitzer, giving the squadron its own integrated artillery support, useful for blinding or knocking out anti-tank guns.

CRUSADER III FEATURES

UP-GUNNED: The 6 pdr gun carried by the Crusader III is a major improvement. At last the British tankers have a weapon with a good chance of defeating the face-hardened armour of the German panzers, even at long range.

IMPROVED PROTECTION: As well as slightly thicker front armour, the Crusader III has improved protection around the turret mounting and the ammunition racks, which were identified as a common cause of fires in the earlier model.

SPECIAL RULES

NO HE: The 2 pdr and 6 pdr guns mounted by the Crusader only have armour-piercing shells. This severely limits its use against infantry and unarmoured targets, as the uncapped solid steel shot will only inflict serious damage with a direct hit to a vital area.

SMOKE: The Crusader CS is designed to act as dedicated artillery support, which includes the ability to fire smoke rounds to blind the enemy.

SMOKE BOMBARDMENT: Laying down a heavy smoke screen can shield the squadron from enemy anti-tank guns while it manoeuvres to attack.

OVERWORKED: The larger 6 pdr gun of the Crusader III restricts turret space, so the commander must also act as the loader, when he should be using every spare moment to observe the tank's surroundings and make crucial tactical decisions. This makes it harder for the crew to fight at top efficiency while on the move.

CRUSADER II

Front Armour: 3
Weapon Range: 24"/60cm
Anti-tank: 7
Firepower: 4+

CRUSADER ARMOURED SQUADRON

CRUSADER ARMOURED TROOP OPTIONS

You can field either a Crusader II Armoured Troop with only 2 pdr-armed Crusader II tanks, or a mixed Troop with both Crusader II tanks and 6 pdr-armed Crusader III tanks.

CRUSADER II ARMOURED TROOP

3x Crusader II (2 pdr) **5 POINTS**

The Crusader entered service in November 1941, in time for Operation Crusader, the offensive in late 1941 that was named after the new tank. Although the Crusader is vulnerable to enemy fire and prone to certain mechanical difficulties, its speed and cross-country manoeuvrability are admired both by its own crews and their German and Italian foes.

• TANK UNIT •

MOTIVATION		SKILL	
CONFIDENT 4+		TRAINED 4+	
Fight Another Day Last Stand	5+	Tally Ho Tactics	5+

IS HIT ON **AGGRESSIVE 3+**

ARMOUR	
FRONT	3
SIDE & REAR	2
TOP	1

TACTICAL	TERRAIN DASH	CROSS COUNTRY DASH	ROAD DASH	CROSS
14"/35cm	14"/35cm	20"/50cm	24"/60cm	3+

WEAPON	RANGE	ROF HALTED	ROF MOVING	ANTI-TANK	FIRE-POWER	NOTES
Crusader II (2 pdr)	24"/60cm	2	1	7	4+	No HE
Crusader II (MG)	16"/40cm	3	3	2	6	

CRUSADER II & III ARMOURED TROOP

1x Crusader II (2 pdr)	
2x Crusader III (6 pdr)	**7 POINTS**
2x Crusader II (2 pdr)	
1x Crusader III (6 pdr)	**6 POINTS**

When the up-gunned Crusader III entered service just prior to the Second Battle of El Alamein, it was eagerly welcomed by the crews. The new tanks are shared out among the squadrons, giving each troop much-needed extra firepower.

• TANK UNIT •

MOTIVATION		SKILL	
CONFIDENT 4+		TRAINED 4+	
Fight Another Day Last Stand	5+	Tally Ho Tactics	5+

IS HIT ON **AGGRESSIVE 3+**

ARMOUR	
CRUSADER II FRONT	3
CRUSADER III FRONT	4
SIDE	2
TOP	1

TACTICAL	TERRAIN DASH	CROSS COUNTRY DASH	ROAD DASH	CROSS
14"/35cm	14"/35cm	20"/50cm	24"/60cm	3+

WEAPON	RANGE	ROF HALTED	ROF MOVING	ANTI-TANK	FIRE-POWER	NOTES
Crusader II (2 pdr)	24"/60cm	2	1	7	4+	No HE
Crusader III (6 pdr)	28"/70cm	2	1	9	4+	No HE, Overworked
Crusader II & III (MG)	16"/40cm	3	3	2	6	

CRUSADERS: ON THE TABLE

There are three different models of Crusader tank.
The key differences are highlighted below to help you pick the right tank for the job.

CRUSADER II CS

Front Armour:	3
Weapon Range:	16"/40cm
Anti-tank:	5
Firepower:	3+
Other:	Artillery Bombardment

CRUSADER III

Front Armour:	4
Weapon Range:	28"/70cm
Anti-tank:	9
Firepower:	4+
Other:	Overworked (+1 To Hit for Moving ROF)

8TH HUSSARS

The 8th King's Royal Irish Hussars were one of the original regiments of the Mobile Force (Egypt) which would go on to form the 7th Armoured Division. The regiment has a long, proud history dating back to the late 17th Century. In the Crimean War, it was one of the regiments which took part in the famous Charge of the Light Brigade, a glorious but costly action which had unfortunate echoes in some of the regiment's Second World War engagements. They began the war in light tanks, fighting through 1940 and 1941 as part of 4 Armoured Brigade, against the Italians and then Rommel's *Afrika Korps*.

Honeys of the 8th Hussars were the first M3 Light Tanks to see combat, against the 5th Panzer Regiment of the 21st Panzer Division near Gabr Saleh, at the start of Operation Crusader on 19 November 1941. It was a harsh baptism of fire, in which the limitations of the lightly armoured tanks quickly became apparent, as the 8th Hussars lost 20 tanks.

But worse was to follow a few days later during the fighting for the Sidi Rezegh airfield. Because tanks are difficult to co-ordinate in the dark, armoured night attacks are rare, and tank units normally consider themselves safe in their night encampments. However, on 22 November, 15th Panzer Division stumbled upon 8th Hussars just as night fell, and were able to surround and overwhelm the regiment. The commander and most of the tanks, along with 4 Armoured Brigade HQ, were captured or destroyed. Only seven of the 8th Hussars' Honey tanks escaped.

The regiment was reformed with new Stuart tanks, and was quickly back in action on December 1, again at Sidi Rezegh. Perhaps the legacy of the Charge of the Light Brigade lived on in the Hussars' memory. Again, they were almost annihilated when they charged 'cavalry style' in support of New Zealand troops. The attack succeeded, but the regiment suffered many casualties, including their new commander.

They were again issued new tanks—this time including two squadrons of Grant tanks. In the defence of Gazala, 4 Armoured Brigade were sent south to meet the *Afrika Korps'* surprise encircling move, and unexpectedly ran straight into the full 15th Panzer Division. They fought bravely, surprising the Germans with their powerful new Grants. However, facing a whole panzer division they took heavy losses and retreated towards El Adem to regroup.

After the retreat from Gazala, the regiment's surviving tanks were temporarily amalgamated with another under-strength light cavalry regiment as the 4th/8th Hussars. This composite regiment fought in the defence of Alam El Halfa at the start of September 1942. They then helped breach the minefields in the Second Battle of El Alamein in October, before joining the pursuit of the retreating Axis forces for the next three weeks.

The 8th Hussars remained with the 7th Armoured Division for the rest of the war, serving as the division's reconnaissance regiment in its long, difficult fight through Normandy, Belgium, the Netherlands, and into Germany itself.

BRIGADES

A brigade consists of three or four regiments or battalions grouped together under a single command. Brigades can operate independently, or two or three brigades can be grouped together into a division.

Brigades are often swapped between divisions as the situation dictates, and battalions are likewise sometimes moved between brigades.

Sometimes two or more battalions which had suffered heavy casualties could be temporarily grouped together into composite units.

HONEY ARMOURED SQUADRON
CRUISER TANK FORMATION

You must field the Formation HQ and one Combat Unit from each black box.
You may also field one Combat Unit from each grey box.

HEADQUARTERS

HONEY ARMOURED SQUADRON HQ
MB106

ARMOUR

HONEY ARMOURED TROOP
MB107

ARMOUR

HONEY ARMOURED TROOP
MB107

GRANT ARMOURED TROOP
MB102

ARMOUR

HONEY ARMOURED TROOP
MB107

ARMOUR

HONEY ARMOURED TROOP
MB107

You may field a Combat Unit from a black box as a Support Unit for another Formation.

Engines idling, the Honeys of C Squadron waited patiently for their slower cousins to catch up. The Grant tanks were rumbling forward at a steady pace, their high profile making them appear slightly top-heavy. As they finally drew level, Major Tom Rutherford, C Squadron commander, gestured and the lighter tanks accelerated away obliquely to the right, the sound of their radial engines fading as the Grants shook out into a line abreast.

The first enemy tanks appeared in the hazy distance and the Grants began firing. Surprised that they could be hit at this range, the panzers split up, some staying to return fire while others moved off towards the flank, executing the tactic that had worked so well for them in the past. This time, though, the Honeys were waiting, and a Mark III panzer, struck in its thinner side armour by a well-placed 37mm shot, began to burn.

The Honeys were loath to sit still and trade shots. They moved at high speed, turrets rotating to follow their targets. In Rutherford's tank, the loader hurriedly fed shells as the gunner poured shot after shot at the enemy tanks. In the rear of the turret, with his head and shoulders protruding through the hexagonal hatch, Rutherford was dangerously exposed, but he knew the unrestricted view of the battlefield was worth it.

HONEY ARMOURED SQUADRON HQ

4x Honey	**7 POINTS**
3x Honey	**5 POINTS**

MOTIVATION
CONFIDENT 4+
Fight Another Day
Last Stand 5+

SKILL
TRAINED 4+
Tally Ho
Tactics 5+

• TANK FORMATION •

IS HIT ON
AGGRESSIVE 3+

ARMOUR
FRONT	👍	3
SIDE & REAR	🛡	2
TOP	⊕	1

The M3 Stuart Light Tank is the first American-made tank supplied to the British Army under the lend-lease programme. One of its intended roles was infantry support. But to the British, infantry tanks are slow and heavily armoured, so the Honey is employed in the same way as the British-built cruisers. Compared with earlier British-designed tanks, it is much less prone to breaking down—so reliable that its drivers call it a 'Honey'.

TACTICAL	TERRAIN DASH	CROSS COUNTRY DASH	ROAD DASH	CROSS
12"/30cm	16"/40cm	24"/60cm	28"/70cm	3+

WEAPON	RANGE	ROF HALTED	ROF MOVING	ANTI-TANK	FIRE-POWER	NOTES
Honey (37mm)	24"/60cm	2	1	7	4+	*No HE*
Honey (MGs)	16"/40cm	5	5	2	6	*Self-defence AA*

HONEY

FEATURES

HIGH TOP SPEED: The Honey is the fastest tank in the British arsenal, outpacing even the Crusaders flat-out. Although British tank doctrine recommended firing on the move, Honey crews found they got their best result through speedily closing with the enemy, quickly halting and then firing their 37mm gun into the side armour of the panzers.

TACTICAL SPEED: Despite its high speed, the M3 Stuart was originally intended for infantry support, so unlike the Crusader, it was not designed with fast-paced moving tank duels in mind. Nevertheless, a few minor modifications have made the Honey a quick and nimble fighter, capable of running circles around its slower adversaries.

SPECIAL RULES

NO HE: British Honeys don't carry high-explosive shells for their 37mm guns. They will need space for as many armour-piercing shells as possible to fight the better-protected German panzers.

SELF-DEFENCE AA: The Honey is equipped with three Browning .30-cal machine-guns: one co-axial with the main gun, one in the bow at the assistant driver's position, and one in an anti-aircraft mount on the turret roof, giving some protection from the Stuka dive bombers.

HONEY ARMOURED TROOP

3x Honey   **5 POINTS**

MOTIVATION		
CONFIDENT 4+		
Fight Another Day ***Last Stand***		**5+**

SKILL		
TRAINED 4+		
Tally Ho ***Tactics***		**5+**

• TANK UNIT •

IS HIT ON	
AGGRESSIVE 3+	

ARMOUR		
FRONT		**3**
SIDE & REAR		**2**
TOP		**1**

TACTICAL	TERRAIN DASH	CROSS COUNTRY DASH	ROAD DASH	CROSS
12"/30CM	16"/40CM	24"/60CM	28"/70CM	3+

WEAPON	RANGE	ROF HALTED	ROF MOVING	ANTI-TANK	FIRE-POWER	NOTES
Honey (37mm)	24"/60CM	2	1	7	4+	*No HE*
Honey (MGs)	16"/40CM	5	5	2	6	*Self-defence AA*

The Honey's armour is not bad for a light tank, but unlike its big brother the Grant, it can't go toe-to-toe with the German panzers—not if its crew want to live for long. With eight forward gears and two reverse, the Honey can get itself out of trouble quickly if it has to.

When they received the M3, the British found many things about its internal layout to be awkward. They quickly made adaptations to improve the tank's usability, including moving the turret traverse controls to the left-hand side, giving control of the turret to the gunner. With space in the turret limited, the tank was designed for the commander to also act as the gunner.

This was far from ideal, because the commander is the tank's eyes and ears, and when operating the gun his vision is too limited to command effectively. The British overcame this by shifting crew functions. In combat, the commander would move to the rear of the turret while the assistant driver would climb up and man the gun.

The German gunners crouched behind their 5cm PaK 38 anti-tank guns, waiting for the British tanks to appear, pursuing the withdrawing panzers into the carefully laid trap. They were caught completely off guard by the sudden appearance of several troops of Honeys on their flank. The light tanks sped diagonally through the gun line, machine-guns blazing from hull and turret. Gun crews fled in terror from the torrents of bullets, bright with tracer rounds. The assault was over in moments, the would-be ambushers scattered just as the Grant tanks began to appear.

Sweeping forward, the Honeys raced to cut off the retreating column of German tanks. One of the Honeys exploded as a 50mm shell hit, penetrated and detonated its fuel tanks. The other small tanks kept moving, using their speed to deny the Afrika Korps tankers an easy target.

One German machine, then another, blossomed into bright fireballs as concentrated fire from the Grants' guns began to strike home. The path of the other panzers' retreat had taken them out of sight in the shelter of a steep-sided wadi. Realising they were too late to prevent the rest of their quarry from escaping back to the safety of their main force, the Honey commander reluctantly signalled his troops to break off the pursuit and regroup. Today's hunt was over, but there would be more battles to come.

THE RIFLE BRIGADE

The Rifle Brigade (Prince Consort's Own) is descended from the famous 95th Rifles of the Napoleonic Wars, who wore dark green jackets in place of the traditional red coat, and were armed with the accurate Baker rifle instead of smooth-bore muskets. This tradition of marksmanship and light-infantry tactics continued into the 20th Century.

The 1st Battalion of the Rifle Brigade (abbreviated 1RB) was one of several battalions of the Rifle Brigade that served with distinction in the North African campaign.

The 1st Battalion began the war as part of the BEF, the British Expeditionary Force in the defence of France, where it was hastily thrown into action in the defence of Calais. The battalion was eventually overwhelmed and captured, but only after a brave stand which held up the German armoured attack for four days, delaying the advance on Dunkirk and helping to save the British Expeditionary Force.

The 1st Battalion was reformed in the United Kingdom and sailed to North Africa as part of 2 Armoured Brigade of the 1st Armoured Division. There it took part in the defence of the Gazala line before joining the retreat to the defensive line at El Alamein.

At the end of June 1942, as the Eighth Army was reorganised to defend the El Alamein line, 1st Battalion was transferred to the 7th Armoured Division, as 22 Armoured Brigade's motor battalion. They would remain with the Desert Rats for the rest of the war.

In the Battle of Alam El Halfa, 22 Armoured Brigade were placed in a defensive line along the southern and eastern slopes of the Alam El Halfa ridge. A major part of the line was flat, unbroken ground—unsuitable for the Grants, with their high profile and hull-mounted gun, but perfect for dug-in and concealed 6-pounder guns. In the first day of fighting, the 1st Battalion's anti-tank platoon claimed 19 enemy tanks destroyed. One gun accounted for five tanks on its own. After night fell, the motor platoons sent out patrols to destroy immobilised tanks to prevent the enemy from recovering them.

The 1st Battalion stayed with 22 Armoured Brigade for the Second Battle of El Alamein and the Tunisia Campaign until May 1943, when the Axis was finally defeated in Africa.

The 1st Battalion was not the only battalion of the Rifle Brigade to fight in North Africa. 2nd and 7th Battalions were with 7 Motor Brigade during the 'crumbling' phase of Operation Lightfoot. 2nd Battalion seized an objective codenamed 'Outpost Snipe' and held it for two days, despite intense bombardment and determined Axis armoured attacks. They destroyed over 50 armoured vehicles with their anti-tank guns and halted a major Axis counterattack. 2nd Battalion's Colonel, Victor Turner, was awarded the Victoria Cross for the action after he fought on despite a head wound, manning a solitary 6 pdr with two other men and destroying several tanks at point-blank range.

1ST BATTALION, THE RIFLE BRIGADE
22 ARMOURED BRIGADE, 7TH ARMOURED DIVISION, OCTOBER 1942

REGIMENT HQ

MOTOR COMPANY HQ
2x 3" Mortars

MOTOR PLATOON
3x Bren Guns
1x Boys anti-tank Rifle
1x 2" Mortar

MOTOR PLATOON
3x Bren Guns
1x Boys anti-tank Rifle
1x 2" Mortar

MACHINE-GUN PLATOON
4x Vickers MMG'S

SCOUT PLATOON
11x Universal carriers
11x Bren Guns
11x Boys Anti-tank Rifles

A COMPANY
C COMPANY
I COMPANY

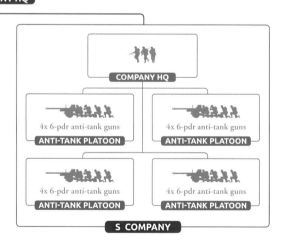

COMPANY HQ

ANTI-TANK PLATOON
4x 6-pdr anti-tank guns

ANTI-TANK PLATOON
4x 6-pdr anti-tank guns

ANTI-TANK PLATOON
4x 6-pdr anti-tank guns

ANTI-TANK PLATOON
4x 6-pdr anti-tank guns

S COMPANY

Unlike the other Battalions of the Rifle Brigade which used the usual A, B C and S (Support) company designations, 1RB consisted of A, C, I and S (Support) Companies. One platoon of four anti-tank guns was usually attached to each Motor Company, with the fourth assigned where it was most needed. Further anti-tank guns could also be attached from the Divisional Support Group if required.

MOTOR COMPANY
INFANTRY FORMATION

You must field the Formation HQ and one Combat Unit from each black box.
You may also field one Combat Unit from each grey box.

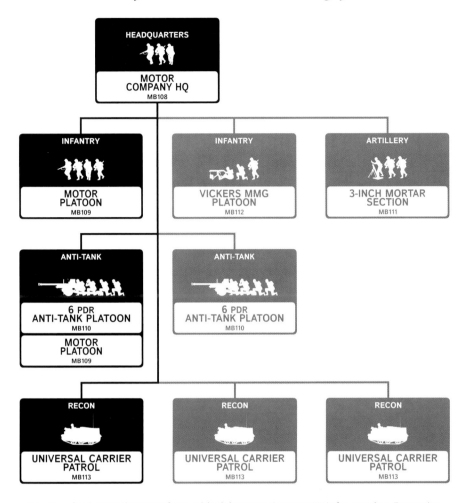

HEADQUARTERS

MOTOR
COMPANY HQ
MB108

INFANTRY

MOTOR
PLATOON
MB109

INFANTRY

VICKERS MMG
PLATOON
MB112

ARTILLERY

3-INCH MORTAR
SECTION
MB111

ANTI-TANK

6 PDR
ANTI-TANK PLATOON
MB110

MOTOR
PLATOON
MB109

ANTI-TANK

6 PDR
ANTI-TANK PLATOON
MB110

RECON

UNIVERSAL CARRIER
PATROL
MB113

RECON

UNIVERSAL CARRIER
PATROL
MB113

RECON

UNIVERSAL CARRIER
PATROL
MB113

You may field a Combat Unit from a black box as a Support Unit for another Formation.

MOTOR COMPANY HQ

2x SMLE rifle team | **2 POINTS**

• INFANTRY FORMATION •

MOTIVATION		IS HIT ON	
CONFIDENT 4+		**CAREFUL 4+**	
Bulldog *Counterattack* **3+**			

SKILL		SAVE	
TRAINED 4+		*Infantry* **3+**	
Deadly *Assault* **3+**			

In the fast-moving environment of the desert war, it is the tanks that usually get all the glory. But the hard work still belongs to the PBI, the 'Poor Bloody Infantry'. For such a small unit, a motor company has plenty of firepower at its disposal. Their machine-guns, anti-tank guns, and mortars can deal with almost any opposition.

TACTICAL	TERRAIN DASH	CROSS COUNTRY DASH	ROAD DASH	CROSS
8"/20cm	8"/20cm	12"/30cm	12"/30cm	AUTO

WEAPON	RANGE	ROF HALTED	ROF MOVING	ANTI-TANK	FIRE-POWER	NOTES
SMLE rifle team	16"/40cm	1	1	2	6	*Slow Firing*

Gunfire crashed around Captain Harker as the Grant tanks of 22 Armoured Brigade, carefully concealed higher up the ridge line, traded shots with the veteran crews of the German tanks—new Mark IV panzers with even more powerful guns. Drifting columns of black smoke showed where combatants had already been reduced to battlefield debris. Neither side had an advantage yet, but the German forces were determined to hunt out the ends of the Allied line so they could once again outflank the British and evict them from their holes. The leading panzers were drawing close to the hidden gun positions of Harker's anti-tank company.

'Steady, lads,' Harker called. 'Let them get just a bit closer.' Gun crews hunkered down behind their 6-pounder anti-tank guns. Dug in, low along the forward slopes of the ridge line, anti-tank guns were devilishly hard for tank crews to spot, peering intently out through tiny vision slits. The angled gun shields were enough to give scant protection from machine-gun fire, but any direct hit from the panzers' main guns would obliterate the gun and the men it sheltered. The gun layers kept one hand on the elevating handwheels, gently traversing the guns with their shoulders to track their chosen target as it drew closer. Loaders crouched, ready to lever open the breech, ejecting the previous spent casing, and slam the next round home.

At last Harker shouted, 'Fire!' Crashing booms rang out as the small guns fired. A panzer shuddered to a sudden halt, its gun drooping. Machine-gun fire quickly began to saturate the area as the panzers returned fire, targeting the clouds of dust thrown up in front of the gun positions. One by one more German tanks stopped, belching fire and smoke as dazed and wounded crew scrambled away from the wrecks. The panzers began to withdraw, still firing, until shimmering heat waves concealed them. The crackling of fires and ammunition cooking off drifted across the suddenly still battlefield. For now, at least, the German attack had failed.

MOTOR PLATOON

4x Bren Gun team
1x Boys anti-tank rifle
1x 2-inch mortar
8 POINTS

3x Bren Gun team
1x Boys anti-tank rifle
1x 2-inch mortar
7 POINTS

The Unit Leader is one of the Bren Gun teams, and is mounted on a small base (see page 44).

Motor platoons spend most of their time forming a safe base for the armour to operate from. On the attack, though, it will be the job of the riflemen to carve a path for the tanks through the enemy defences.

• INFANTRY UNIT •

MOTIVATION		IS HIT ON	
CONFIDENT 4+		**CAREFUL 4+**	
Bulldog Counterattack 3+			

SKILL		SAVE	
TRAINED 4+		*Infantry* **3+**	
Deadly Assault 3+			

TACTICAL	TERRAIN DASH	CROSS COUNTRY DASH	ROAD DASH	CROSS
8"/20CM	8"/20CM	12"/30CM	12"/30CM	AUTO

WEAPON	RANGE	ROF HALTED	ROF MOVING	ANTI-TANK	FIRE-POWER	NOTES
Bren Gun team	16"/40CM	3	2	2	6	
Boys anti-tank rifle	20"/50CM	1	1	4	5+	Assault 4+, Slow Firing
2-inch mortar	16"/40CM	1	1	2	4+	Assault 4+, Overhead Fire, Slow Firing, Smoke

MOTOR COMPANY WEAPONS

SMLE RIFLE: The motor company HQ are mostly concerned with directing the platoons under their command. They only carry slower-firing weapons like the .303-calibre Short Magazine Lee–Enfield (SMLE, aka. 'Smelly'), a reliable and accurate weapon but slow firing compared to the Bren gun.

BREN GUN: The motor platoon's main firepower comes from its accurate and reliable .303-calibre Bren light machine-guns. Each rifleman carries four spare magazines for his section's Bren in two chest pouches on his webbing gear, and each is trained to use the Bren gun if necessary.

BOYS ANTI-TANK RIFLE: The slow-firing .55-calibre bolt-action Boys anti-tank rifle is too cumbersome to use easily on the move. It is best fired prone, using its bipod.

2-INCH MORTAR: The SBML (smooth-bore muzzle-loading) 2-inch mortar conducts overhead fire, throwing a 1kg (2lb) high-explosive bomb in an arcing trajectory, down onto the heads of the enemy. It can also fire rounds that use white phosphorous or titanium tetrachloride to produce dense, white smoke to block the enemy's vision. It must be fired from a firm position on the ground, so is slow firing.

ASSAULT 4+: The crews of the 2-inch mortar and the Boys anti-tank rifle are not as well equipped as the riflemen for hand-to-hand combat, so they hit on a score of 4+ rather than 3+ in assaults.

6 PDR ANTI-TANK PLATOON

4x 6 pdr gun **12 POINTS**
3x 6 pdr gun **9 POINTS**
2x 6 pdr gun **6 POINTS**

The Quick-Firing 6-pounder is a 57mm anti-tank gun which made its combat debut in the Gazala battles in May and June 1942. Dug-in and firing at only point blank range, these guns are deadly to enemy tanks.

• GUN UNIT • GUN SHIELD •

MOTIVATION		IS HIT ON	
FEARLESS 3+		**CAREFUL 4+**	

SKILL		SAVE	
VETERAN 3+		*Gun* **3+**	
Gun Assault 4+			

TACTICAL	TERRAIN DASH	CROSS COUNTRY DASH	ROAD DASH	CROSS
2"/5CM	2"/5CM	4"/10CM	4"/10CM	5+

WEAPON	RANGE	ROF HALTED	ROF MOVING	ANTI-TANK	FIRE-POWER	NOTES
6 pdr gun	28"/70CM	2	1	9	4+	Forward Firing, No HE

6 POUNDER

FEATURES

ARMOUR PENETRATION: The 6 pdr's high-velocity solid armour-piercing rounds can punch through the armour of all but the heaviest German panzers.

GUN SHIELD: The best defence is to wait in concealment until the perfect time to fire. The bulletproof gun shield does give the gun crew some welcome protection, though.

SPECIAL RULES

FORWARD FIRING: The trail does not allow the 6 pdr gun to traverse quickly to track targets moving to its sides, so it can only fire at targets to its front.

NO HE: Although a high-explosive shell has been designed for the 6 pdr, Britain's limited production resources are being concentrated on crucial armour-piercing rounds.

UNIVERSAL CARRIER PATROL

3x Universal Carriers | **2 POINTS**

OPTIONS
- Arm any or all Universal Carriers with a Boys AT rifle for +1 point for the Unit.

• TANK UNIT • SCOUT • SPEARHEAD •

MOTIVATION	
CONFIDENT	**4+**
Scout Counterattack	6
Scout Last Stand	5+

SKILL	
TRAINED	**4+**
Scout Assault	5+

IS HIT ON	
CAREFUL	**4+**

ARMOUR		
FRONT		1
SIDE & REAR		0
TOP		0

TACTICAL	TERRAIN DASH	CROSS COUNTRY DASH	ROAD DASH	CROSS
10"/25CM	14"/35CM	20"/50CM	24"/60CM	4+

WEAPON	RANGE	ROF HALTED	MOVING	ANTI-TANK	FIRE-POWER	NOTES
Carrier (MG)	16"/40CM	3	3	2	6	*Forward Firing*
Optional Carrier (Boys AT rifle)	20"/50CM	1	1	4	5+	*Forward Firing, Slow Firing*

Each motor company includes a scout platoon of Universal Carriers. This versatile vehicle is commonly called a Bren Gun Carrier, which was the first variant developed, even though it has since evolved into a more general-purpose vehicle. Their usual job is scouting No Man's Land to reconnoitre enemy positions.

They are also good for protecting the motor company's flanks as a mobile reserve, delivering extra firepower where it is most needed.

UNIVERSAL CARRIER

FEATURES

ARMOURED CARRIER: The scout platoon's carriers give them the mobility they need to roam far out into No-Man's-Land, and their humble armour protection is hopefully enough to let them survive contact with the enemy and report back.

OPEN SCOUT: The Universal Carrier is meant for reconnaissance and transport, not to be used as an assault vehicle. It is not built for up-close engagements. Its unprotected top makes a tempting target for a hand grenade or spray of submachine-gun fire.

SPECIAL RULES

SCOUT: Small and quick, with a low profile, the Universal Carrier is well suited to the task of reconnaissance, sneaking forward to observe the enemy, then speeding away if spotted.

SPEARHEAD: By scouting ahead and providing up-to-date reports on enemy movements, the scout platoon lets the combat elements know exactly how far they can advance before meeting the first line of enemy defences.

3-INCH MORTAR SECTION

2x 3-inch mortar	**3 POINTS**

MOTIVATION			IS HIT ON	
CONFIDENT 4+			**CAREFUL 4+**	
SKILL		• INFANTRY UNIT • HEAVY WEAPON •	SAVE	
TRAINED 4+			Infantry	**3+**
Heavy Weapon Assault **5+**				

Each motor company has a section of two 3-inch mortars for close support. They fire a 5kg (10lb) high-explosive bomb which can knock out enemy gun positions or break up attacking infantry units. While not as deadly as its big-barrelled Royal Artillery counterparts, the 3-inch mortar is a more portable alternative.

TACTICAL	TERRAIN DASH	CROSS COUNTRY DASH	ROAD DASH	CROSS
4"/10CM	4"/10CM	6"/15CM	8"/20CM	3+

WEAPON	RANGE	ROF HALTED	MOVING	ANTI-TANK	FIRE-POWER	NOTES
3-inch mortar	32"/80CM	ARTILLERY		1	4+	*Smoke Bombardment*

3-INCH MORTAR FEATURES

ARTILLERY: Mortar bombs fly in a high-arcing trajectory, soaring over friendly troops and intervening terrain, to drop down onto the target from above. Unlike most other infantry weapons, they cannot conduct direct fire.

SMOKE BOMBARDMENT: When the enemy cannot see you, they cannot hurt you. Where there is no terrain features to conceal your movements, laying down a dense, blinding smokescreen is the next best thing.

VICKERS MMG PLATOON

4x Vickers MMG team	**4 POINTS**
2x Vickers MMG team	**2 POINTS**

MOTIVATION			IS HIT ON	
CONFIDENT 4+			**CAREFUL 4+**	
Bulldog Counterattack **3+**		• INFANTRY UNIT • HEAVY WEAPON •	SAVE	
SKILL			Infantry	**3+**
TRAINED 4+				
Heavy Weapon Assault **5+**				

Machine-guns used to be grouped together in the battalion support company, but by 1942 each motor company has its own attached machine-gun platoon. The Vickers medium machine-guns pin the enemy down while the motor platoons manoeuvre for the knock-out blow. On the defensive, no enemy infantry can approach the Vickers without weathering a storm of lead.

TACTICAL	TERRAIN DASH	CROSS COUNTRY DASH	ROAD DASH	CROSS
8"/20CM	8"/20CM	12"/30CM	12"/30CM	AUTO

WEAPON	RANGE	ROF HALTED	MOVING	ANTI-TANK	FIRE-POWER	NOTES
Vickers MMG team	24"/60CM	6	2	2	6	
Firing Bombardment	48"/120CM	ARTILLERY		1	6	

VICKERS MMG FEATURES

HIGH RATE OF FIRE: The belt-fed, water-cooled Vickers gun is an extremely reliable weapon, able to fire continuously for hours without jamming. Firing up to 500 rounds per minute, the hail of lead it throws out makes a frontal assault a deadly proposition for any unarmoured enemy.

ARTILLERY: When the Vickers was first used in the First World War, machine-gunners devised a technique of firing high-angle barrages of long-range indirect fire against enemy positions up to several miles away. The bullets strike the area without warning, a silent killer for any infantry unprotected in the open.

SUPPORT UNITS

B Troop's Gun Position Officer bent over a portable table, marking targets and calculating ranges. Signaller Little knelt beside him, engaged in a steady monotone conversation with other radio operators on the net. As soon as the first fire mission was ready, bearing and elevation were passed to the guns. The din of war commenced as the guns fired, crashing back in their cradles, breeches flying open to eject spent propellant cartridges. The gunners worked in a steady rhythm, ramming home shells and cartridges. Far down range, explosions began to fountain on the desert floor. German infantry of the 90th Light Africa Division were engulfed in shrapnel and rock splinters as high-explosive rounds detonated all around them, taking a terrible toll on the exposed soldiers.

Further to the west, 7 Motor Brigade spotted a patrol of eight-wheeled German armoured cars trying to sweep around their flank, prompting a new fire mission. Back at the battery, the gun layers heaved up the tail end of the carriages, smoothly rotating the guns on the firing platforms. The new firing solution came in and within moments the guns resumed. Soon the armoured cars were retreating, leaving several of their vehicles behind as smoking wreckage.

25 PDR FIELD TROOP

4x 25 pdr gun	**14 POINTS**
2x 25 pdr gun	**7 POINTS**

MOTIVATION
FEARLESS 3+

SKILL
VETERAN 3+
Gun **Assault** 4+

• GUN UNIT • GUN SHIELD •
• LARGE GUN • MIKE TARGET •

IS HIT ON
CAREFUL 4+

SAVE
Gun **4+**

The versatile Quick-Firing 25-pounder entered service just before the war began, and remains the main British field gun and howitzer throughout the desert war.

Its main ammunition is an 11.5kg (25lb) 87.6mm high-explosive shell, with solid armour-piercing rounds also available.

TACTICAL	TERRAIN DASH	CROSS COUNTRY DASH	ROAD DASH	CROSS
-	2"/5CM	4"/10CM	4"/10CM	6

WEAPON	RANGE	ROF HALTED	ROF MOVING	ANTI-TANK	FIRE-POWER	NOTES
25 pdr gun	80"/200CM	ARTILLERY		3	4+	Smoke Bombardment
or Direct Fire	24"/60CM	2	1	9	3+	Smoke

25 PDR FEATURES

DUAL PURPOSE: The open, mobile nature of desert warfare sometimes sees tanks and guns coming into close contact, with the 25 pdrs direct-firing at enemy tanks over open sights. Each gun is supplied with solid steel armour-piercing rounds for this eventuality.

FEARLESS: The Royal Artillery gunners are staunch in the face of danger, and will only ever abandon their guns with extreme reluctance, even after taking heavy casualties.

LONG-RANGE ARTILLERY: While the 25 pdr is of some use in anti-tank work, it excels in its primary role as a field gun. It can fire to a range of over 12km (7.5 miles), threatening distant enemy infantry, guns, and even tanks.

TURNTABLE: A circular firing platform attached underneath the trail is lowered to the ground and the gun is pulled onto it. This provides a stable surface on which the gun can quickly be rotated in any direction.

HONEY OP OBSERVATION POST

1x Honey OP	**2 POINTS**

You must field a 25 pdr Field Troop (MB116) before you can field a Honey OP.

MOTIVATION
CONFIDENT 4+
Scout **Last Stand** 6
Observer **Counterattack** 5+

SKILL
VETERAN 3+

• TANK UNIT • INDEPENDENT •
• OBSERVER • SCOUT •

IS HIT ON
CAREFUL 4+

ARMOUR
FRONT 3
SIDE & REAR 2
TOP 1

The 25 pdrs can accurately send shells 12km (7.5 miles) but they are blind without a forward observation post to direct the bombardment. To keep up with the armoured units, the FOO (Forward Observation Officer) and his team have their own tank.

TACTICAL	TERRAIN DASH	CROSS COUNTRY DASH	ROAD DASH	CROSS
10"/25CM	16"/40CM	24"/60CM	28"/70CM	3+

WEAPON	RANGE	ROF HALTED	ROF MOVING	ANTI-TANK	FIRE-POWER	NOTES
Honey OP (37mm)	24"/60CM	1	1	7	4+	No HE
Honey OP (MGs)	16"/40CM	5	5	2	6	Self-defence AA

SUPPORT UNITS

17 PDR ANTI-TANK TROOP

4x 17/25 pdr gun — **16 POINTS**
3x 17/25 pdr gun — **12 POINTS**
2x 17/25 pdr gun — **8 POINTS**

MOTIVATION		IS HIT ON
FEARLESS 3+	• GUN UNIT • GUN SHIELD • LARGE GUN •	**CAREFUL** 4+

SKILL		SAVE
VETERAN 3+		**4+**
Gun Assault 4+		*Gun*

TACTICAL	TERRAIN DASH	CROSS COUNTRY DASH	ROAD DASH	CROSS
-	2"/5CM	4"/10CM	4"/10CM	6

WEAPON	RANGE	ROF HALTED	ROF MOVING	ANTI-TANK	FIRE-POWER	NOTES
17/25 pdr gun	36"/90CM	2	1	12	3+	*Forward Firing, No HE*

In the ongoing race between tank armour and anti-tank guns, even the 6 pdr would not be powerful enough for long. The answer was the huge 17-pounder. The barrel was ready by May 1942, but the carriage still needed work, so in an effort to rush the gun into service to deal with the arrival of heavy German panzers like the Tiger, a temporary hybrid solution was created by mounting the gun on a 25 pdr carriage.

The resulting 17/25-pounder, codenamed the 'Pheasant', first saw action at the Battle of Medenine in March 1943.

17 PDR FEATURES

LONG RANGE: The 17/25-pounder is a large and imposing gun. Its barrel is almost 4.2m (13' 9") long, giving it a high muzzle velocity and good long-range accuracy. Its size makes it harder to conceal than smaller anti-tank guns.

UNRIVALLED PENETRATION: Even at long range, the solid armour-piercing round fired by the 17/25 pdr is more than a match for the armour of the German panzers. Even the mighty Tiger will be lucky to survive a direct hit.

HUMBER ARMOURED CAR TROOP

3x Humber   **3 POINTS**

MOTIVATION	
CONFIDENT 4+	
Scout Counterattack	6
Scout Last Stand	5+

SKILL	
VETERAN 3+	
Scout Assault	4+

• TANK UNIT • SCOUT • SPEARHEAD •

IS HIT ON	
CAREFUL 4+	

ARMOUR		
FRONT		1
SIDE & REAR		1
TOP		0

TACTICAL	TERRAIN DASH	CROSS COUNTRY DASH	ROAD DASH	CROSS
8"/20CM	10"/25CM	14"/35CM	32"/80CM	4+

WEAPON	RANGE	ROF HALTED	ROF MOVING	ANTI-TANK	FIRE-POWER	NOTES
Humber (15mm)	20"/50CM	3	2	5	5+	
Humber (MG)	16"/40CM	3	3	2	6	

Armoured cars play a similar role to the light cavalry regiments of old, roaming far ahead of the tanks, observing enemy dispositions and reporting their movements. In pursuits they lead the chase, harassing the retreating enemy and ambushing fleeing convoys. In retreats they are the rearguard, slowing the enemy advance and covering the withdrawal of the fighting forces.

The Humber is one of the most successful British armoured car designs. While its real job is reconnaissance, its 15mm Besa machine-gun poses a serious danger to lightly armoured targets.

The Humber is fielded in North Africa by several cavalry units, including the 11th Hussars, one of the units that cut off the retreating Italian Tenth Army at Beda Fomm back in 1940.

HUMBER FEATURES

SCOUT: The job of reconnaissance units is not to stand and fight, but to provide information about enemy movements. They are adept at avoiding detection and getting away quickly if spotted. Light wheeled vehicles aren't tanks—they don't have the weight to simply crush infantry positions, making direct assaults a much more dicey proposition.

SPEARHEAD: Once the recce units have ascertained the strength and dispersal of the enemy, the information they pass back to the combat elements lets them know exactly where they can safely push forward without undue risk.

BOFORS LIGHT AA TROOP

| 6x Bofors 40mm AA gun | **8 POINTS** |
| 3x Bofors 40mm AA gun | **4 POINTS** |

MOTIVATION
CONFIDENT 4+

SKILL
VETERAN 3+
Gun Assault 4+

• GUN UNIT • LARGE GUN •

IS HIT ON
CAREFUL 4+

SAVE
Gun 4+

The open desert offers precious little cover from the Stuka dive-bombers of the Luftwaffe. The quick-firing Bofors guns can be relied on to drive away the harassing Axis aircraft before they have a chance to do too much harm.

TACTICAL	TERRAIN DASH	CROSS COUNTRY DASH	ROAD DASH	CROSS
-	2"/5CM	4"/10CM	4"/10CM	6

WEAPON	RANGE	ROF HALTED	ROF MOVING	ANTI-TANK	FIRE-POWER	NOTES
Bofors 40mm AA gun	24"/60CM	3	2	7	4+	Dedicated AA

HURRICANE TANK-BUSTING FLIGHT

| 2x Hurricane | **9 POINTS** |

MOTIVATION
CONFIDENT 4+

SKILL
TRAINED 4+

• AIRCRAFT UNIT •

IS HIT ON
AIRCRAFT 5+

SAVE
Aircraft 3+

Based on the Royal Air Force's most numerous single-seat fighter, the Hawker IID tank buster is nicknamed the 'Flying Can Opener'. A Vickers S gun beneath each wing fires 40mm armour-piercing ammunition. Each is mounted under a machine-gun firing tracer rounds to aid with sighting, making them accurate and deadly.

TACTICAL	TERRAIN DASH	CROSS COUNTRY DASH	ROAD DASH	CROSS
	UNLIMITED			AUTO

WEAPON	RANGE	ROF HALTED	ROF MOVING	ANTI-TANK	FIRE-POWER	NOTES
Hurricane (Vickers S gun)	8"/20CM	-	2	7	4+	

PAINTING DESERT RATS

ARMOUR COLOURS

CRUSADER
DESERT PINK & DARK OLIVE GREEN

GRANT
FOUR-COLOUR PATTERN

HONEY
LIGHT STONE NO. 61

A number of camouflage concepts were trialled by the British army for the desert. From late 1941, through most of 1942, an all-over basic colour of *Light Stone No. 61* (Crusader Sand), a pale dull yellow, was used on all vehicles and artillery.

In October 1942, prior to the Second Battle of El Alamein, new orders were issued changing the basic colour to *Desert Pink* (DAK Sand), with a disruptive pattern of Dark Olive Green (Firefly Green)

The instructions applied to new and repaired vehicles, so many tanks at El Alamein were still in plain Light Stone.

Grant tanks arrived from the US in their original Olive Drab colour, which was usually painted over with Light Stone, sometimes leaving Olive Drab areas as a disruptive pattern.

A few regiments outlined the edges of the camouflage pattern with black and white lines.

DESERT RATS ARMOUR

COLOUR PALETTE

CRUSADER SAND
(363)

ROMMEL SHADE
(494)

DRY DUST
(364)

Pale colours like Crusader Sand, the most common colour for British desert tanks, can be challenging to paint over a dark base without getting ugly brush strokes. Consider using a white or pale grey primer to make it easier to get a bright, even finish.

Crusader Sand is also available as a spray can, the quickest and easiest way to basecoat your tanks.

CRUSADER SAND
Large Brush

BASECOAT *your tank with Crusader Sand. Two thin coats are better than one thick coat.*

ROMMEL SHADE
Large Brush

WASH *the tank with Rommel Shade. Try to achieve an even coverage over the whole tank, letting the wash pool in the recesses without building up too much on flat surfaces.*

CRUSADER SAND
Medium Brush

TIDY UP *the wash with Crusader Sand using a combination of drybrushing and layering.*

DRY DUST
Small Drybrush

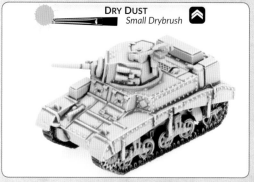

DRYBRUSH *the tank with Dry Dust, concentrating on edges, raised details, and upper surfaces to add highlights.*

TANK CAMOUFLAGE

COLOUR PALETTE

DAK SAND
(366)

FIREFLY GREEN
(348)

ROMMEL SHADE
(494)

DRY DUST
(364)

The tanks that fought in the Second Battle of El Alamein typically had a two-colour disruptive camouflage pattern.

Desert Pink was chosen as the basic colour. It was thought that its light earthy tone would blend well into the terrain of most parts of the Western Desert.

The disruptive pattern was intended to make it harder for the enemy to identify specific vehicle types, rather than to truly hide the vehicle from sight.

Sometimes, when Dark Olive Green was not available, black or dark brown was substituted.

DAK SAND — *Large Brush*

BASECOAT *your tank with DAK Sand. Two thin coats are preferable to one thick coat, and you may find it easier if you use a white or light grey undercoat.*

FIREFLY GREEN — *Large Brush*

PAINT *Cloud-shaped patches of Firefly Green, concentrating mainly on the lower parts of the tank. Road wheels should be all be one solid colour.*

ROMMEL SHADE — *Large Brush*

WASH *the tank with Rommel Shade to add shading. You can substitute Bradley Shade if you have it, to emphasise the warmer tone of the Desert Pink base colour.*

DAK SAND — *Medium Brush*

TIDY UP *the wash with DAK Sand using a combination of drybrushing and layering, leaving darker shading in recessed areas.*

FIREFLY GREEN — *Medium Brush*

TIDY UP *the disruptive camouflage areas in a similar way using Firefly Green.*

DRY DUST — *Small Drybrush*

DRYBRUSH *the tank with Dry Dust, concentrating on edges, raised details, and upper surfaces to add highlights and give the tank a weathered, dusty finish.*

TANK TRACKS

COLOUR PALETTE

MOTHERLAND EARTH
(383)

ROMMEL SHADE
(494)

DARK GUNMETAL
(480)

MOTHERLAND EARTH — *Medium Brush*

BASECOAT *the tracks Motherland Earth or Battlefield Brown.*

ROMMEL SHADE — *Medium Brush*

WASH *with Rommel Shade to enhance shading. You can substitute Manstein Shade for a darker result.*

DARK GUNMETAL — *Small Drybrush*

DRYBRUSH *the tracks with Dark gunmetal. Note, Honey and Grant track links have solid rubber pads.*

DESERT RATS TANK MARKINGS

Tactical markings are an excellent way of adding visual and historical interest to your models. British tanks had a divisional symbol on the left-hand mudguards, and a regimental number on the right. A geometric symbol on the sides of the turret identified the squadron. You can find more information on British markings in *Colours Of War* and on the *Flames Of War* website.

SQUADRON MARKINGS

△	□	○
A **Squadron**	*B* **Squadron**	*C* **Squadron**

Each tank in a squadron will have the same turret marking. The shape shows the squadron, while the colour—red, yellow or blue—denotes its regiment.

Regiment Number

Divisional Symbol

Squadron Marking

Divisional Symbol

1ST ARMOURED DIVSION
The Desert Rats were not the only British armoured division to serve in the desert. 1ST Armoured Division arrived in May 1942.

Regiment Number

Most unit boxes come with the decal sheet shown here. More decal options can be found on BR940 British Desert Rats Decal Sheet.

DESERT RATS INFANTRY

British troops in North Africa wore a uniform consisting of khaki drill shorts or slacks with long-sleeved Aertex shirts.

The light khaki drill fabric was good in the hot desert sun, but was usually insufficient for the cold desert nights.

Webbing equipment was simple raw canvas, not treated with Blanco, the coloured cleaning paste which uniform regulations required for troops in other theatres.

Metal items such as brass buckles were left unpolished to reduce potential glare.

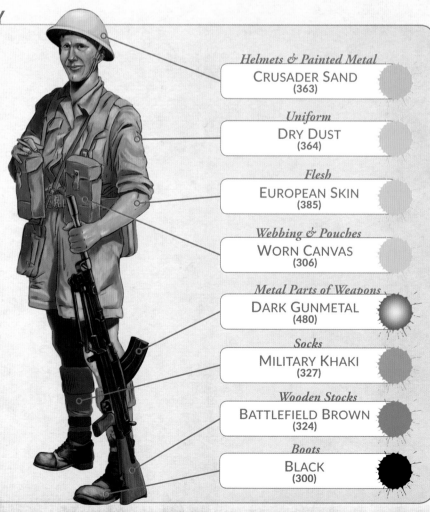

Helmets & Painted Metal
CRUSADER SAND
(363)

Uniform
DRY DUST
(364)

Flesh
EUROPEAN SKIN
(385)

Webbing & Pouches
WORN CANVAS
(306)

Metal Parts of Weapons
DARK GUNMETAL
(480)

Socks
MILITARY KHAKI
(327)

Wooden Stocks
BATTLEFIELD BROWN
(324)

Boots
BLACK
(300)

UNIFORMS AND WEBBING

COLOUR PALETTE

DRY DUST
(364)

WORN CANVAS
(306)

MILITARY KHAKI
(327)

ROMMEL SHADE
(494)

The paler shade of the khaki drill tropical uniform was better suited to desert regions than the heavy brown serge of standard Battledress.

DRY DUST *Medium Brush*

BASECOAT *the uniform with Dry Dust, using multiple thin coats if necessary to get an even coverage.*

WORN CANVAS *Small Brush*

BASECOAT *the webbing gear and rifle slings with Worn Canvas.*

MILITARY KHAKI *Medium Brush*

BASECOAT *the socks with Military Khaki.*

ROMMEL SHADE *Medium Brush*

WASH *the figure liberally with Rommel Shade to add realistic shading.*

DRY DUST *Small Brush*

ACTUAL SIZE

HIGHLIGHT *the uniform with Dry Dust, concentrating on folds and raised details.*

FLESH

EUROPEAN SKIN
(385)

SKIN SHADE
(491)

You can find more advanced methods for painting flesh on page 23 of *Colours Of War.*

EUROPEAN SKIN *Medium Brush*

BASECOAT *the face and other exposed skin areas with European Skin, in two thin coats.*

SKIN SHADE *Medium Brush*

WASH *liberally with Skin Shade to create shading and definition.*

EUROPEAN SKIN *Small Brush*

ACTUAL SIZE

HIGHLIGHT *prominent details such as fingers, cheeks and nose with European Skin.*

WEAPONS

DARK GUNMETAL
(480)

BATTLEFIELD BROWN
(324)

SKIN SHADE
(491)

DARK GUNMETAL *Medium Brush*

PAINT *barrels and other metal parts sparingly with Dark Gunmetal.*

BATTLEFIELD BROWN *Medium Brush*

BASECOAT *stocks and other wooden areas with Battlefield Brown.*

SKIN SHADE *Medium Brush*

ACTUAL SIZE

WASH *with Skin Shade to add shading and deepen the wood colour.*

Aircraft

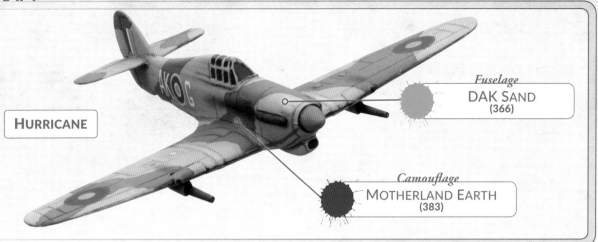

HURRICANE

Fuselage
DAK SAND
(366)

Camouflage
MOTHERLAND EARTH
(383)

Basing Guide

All *Flames Of War* infantry and guns are supplied with appropriate bases. Assemble your infantry teams by gluing the figures into the holes on a base of the right size. Super glue works well for this.

There are usually several figures with each type of weapon, so you can create variety in your teams. It doesn't matter which mix of figures you put in each team, as long as the mix of weapons is right. Visit the product spotlight on the *Flames Of War* website: www.FlamesOfWar.com for a more detailed guide.

Commanders and Unit Leaders

Base the Motor Company HQ teams and the Motor Platoon Unit Leader on a small base with an NCO and a rifleman. The team faces the long edge.

Bren Gun team

Base the Bren Gun teams of a Motor Platoon on a medium base. Teams combine a gunner armed with a Bren light machine-gun, an NCO, and two riflemen armed with Lee Enfield rifles. The team faces the long edge.

Vickers MMG   *3-inch mortar*

Base these heavy weapons on medium base facing the long edge. These teams have the gunner and his weapon along with two assistant gunners or loaders.

Boys anti-tank rifle   *2-inch mortar*

Base Boys anti-tank rifles and 2-inch mortars on a small base with a rifleman loader. The team faces the long edge.

6 pdr gun

Base the 6 pdr gun on a medium base facing the short edge. Each gun has a gunner along with an NCO and two ammunition loaders.

17/25 pdr gun

25 pdr gun

Bofors 40mm AA gun

Base these guns on a large base facing the short edge. Each 25 pdr and 17/25 pdr gun has a gunner along with an NCO and three ammunition loaders. The Bofors has two gunners, an NCO and an ammunition loader.

MONTY'S DESERT RATS

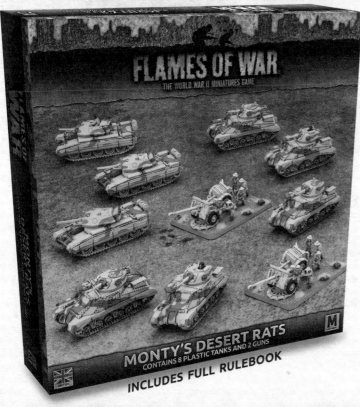

Monty's Desert Rats is the best starting point for any British Desert army.

Expand your force by adding other units from the Britsh range. Each Flames Of War unit box contains a complete unit and their Unit Cards.

BRAB09	Monty's Desert Rats *(x5 Grant, x3 Crusader, x2 17pdr) (Plastic)*	
BBX32	Honey Armoured Troop *(x5) (Plastic)*	
BBX33	25pdr Field Troop *(x4) (Plastic)*	
BBX35	Universal Carrier Patrol *(x9) (Plastic)*	
BBX37	Grant Armoured Troop *(x5) (Plastic)*	
BBX38	6pdr Anti-tank Platoon *(x4) (Plastic)*	
BBX39	Crusader Armoured Troop *(x5) (Plastic)*	
BBX41	17/25pdr Anti-Tank Troop *(x2) (Plastic)*	
BR753	Motor Platoon *(x26 figures) (Plastic)*	
BR754	MMG Platoon & Mortar Section *(x4 HMG, x2 3" Mortars) (Plastic)*	
BBX34	Humber Armoured Car Troop *(x3)*	
BBX36	Bofors Light AA Troop *(x3)*	
BBX40	Hurricane Tank-Busting Flight *(x2)*	
BR900	Desert Rats Dice *(x20)*	
BR901	Desert Rats Tokens *(x20)*	
CWP131	Desert Rats Paint Set *(x5 paints)*	
CWP231	Desert Rats Spray *(Crusader Sand)*	

17 PDR ANTI-TANK TROOP

HONEY ARMOURED TROOP
CONTAINS 5 PLASTIC HONEY TANKS

DESERT RATS PAINT SET

25 PDR FIELD TROOP
CONTAINS 4 PLASTIC GUNS

CRUSADER ARMOURED TROOP
CONTAINS 5 PLASTIC CRUSADER TANKS

For more information visit our website: www.flamesofwar.com